# CHARLES RAY

VIRAL RESEARCH, 1986

3

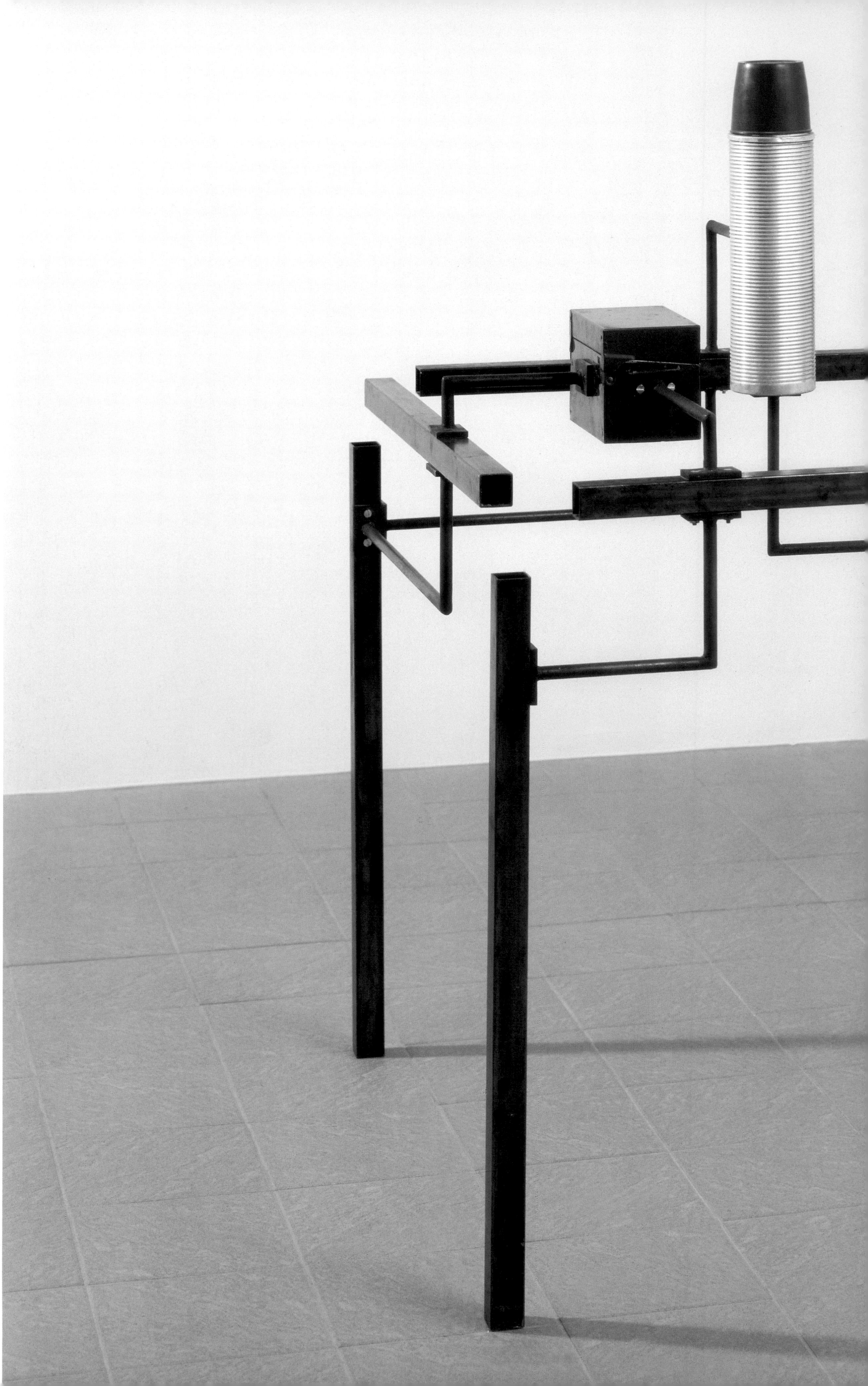

HOW A TABLE WORKS, 1986

TUB WITH BLACK DYE, 1986

INK BOX, 1986

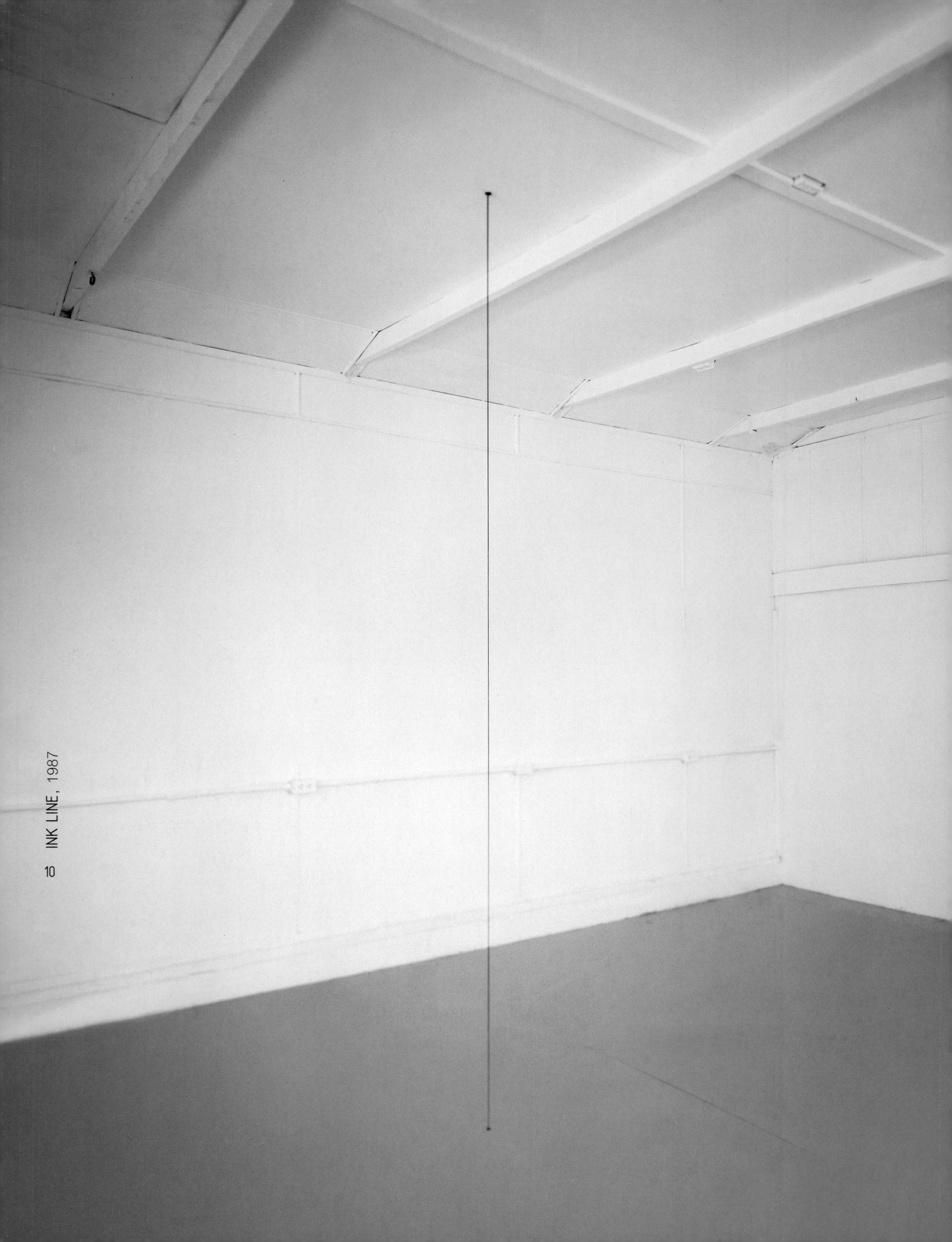



INK LINE, 1987

ROTATING CIRCLE, 1988

13

14    BATH, 1989

17   32x33x35=34,x33x35, 1989

SELF-PORTRAIT, 1990

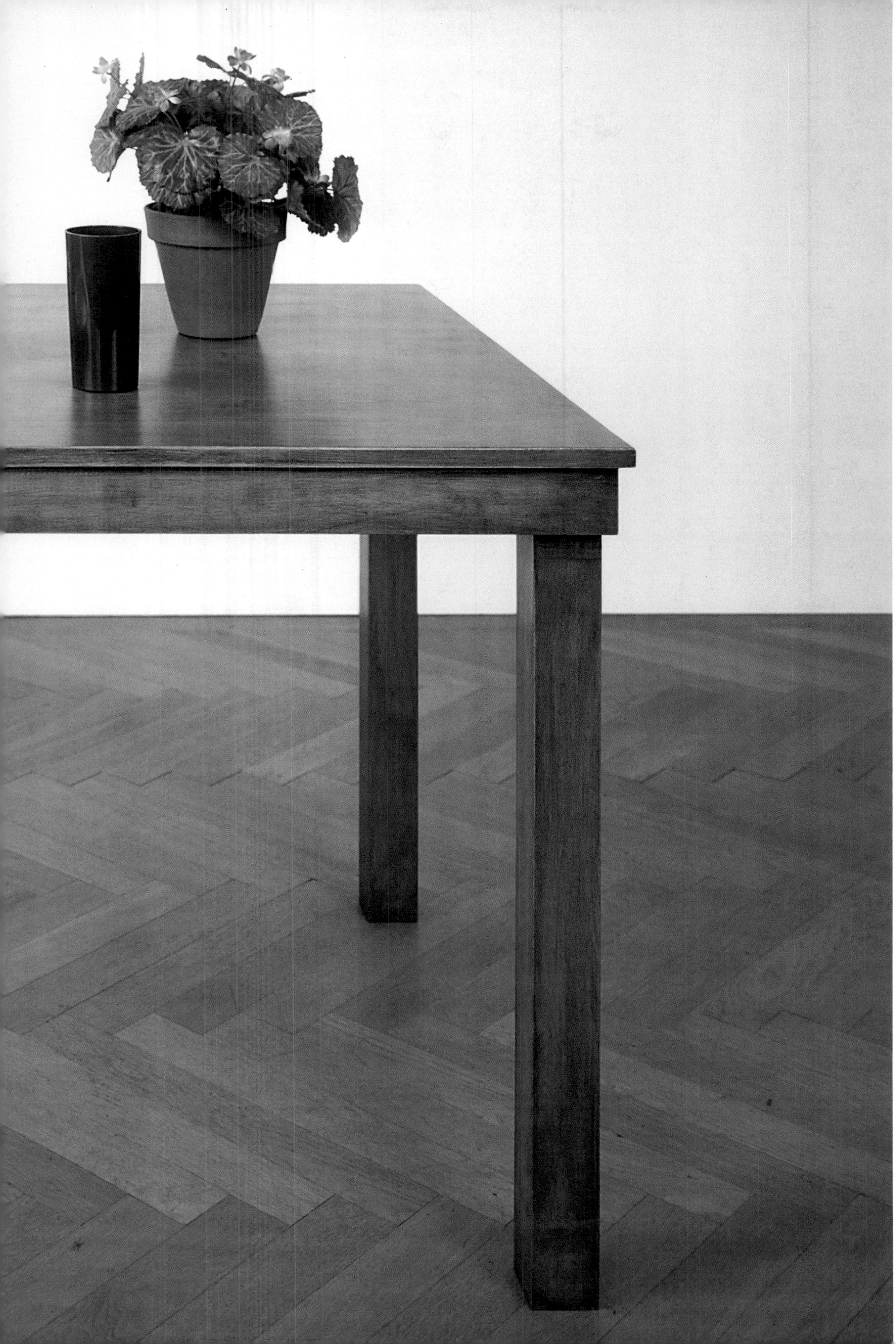

21 TABLETOP, 1988

YES, 1990

22

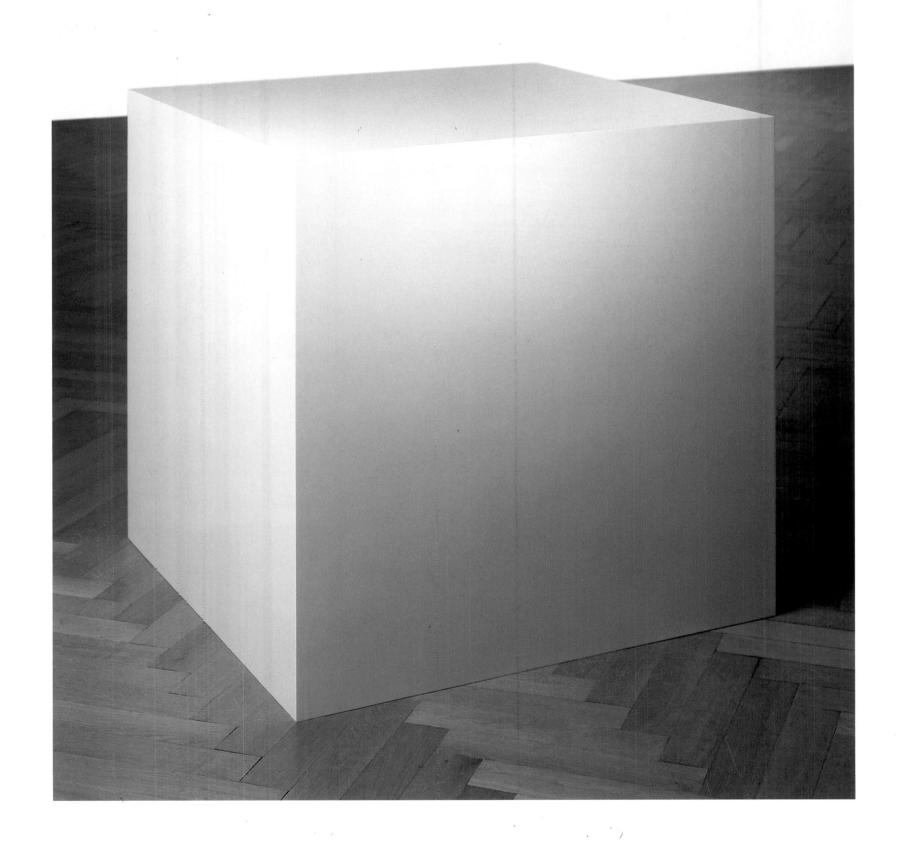

7½-TON CUBE, 1990

23

MALE MANNEQUIN, 1990

FALL '91, 1992

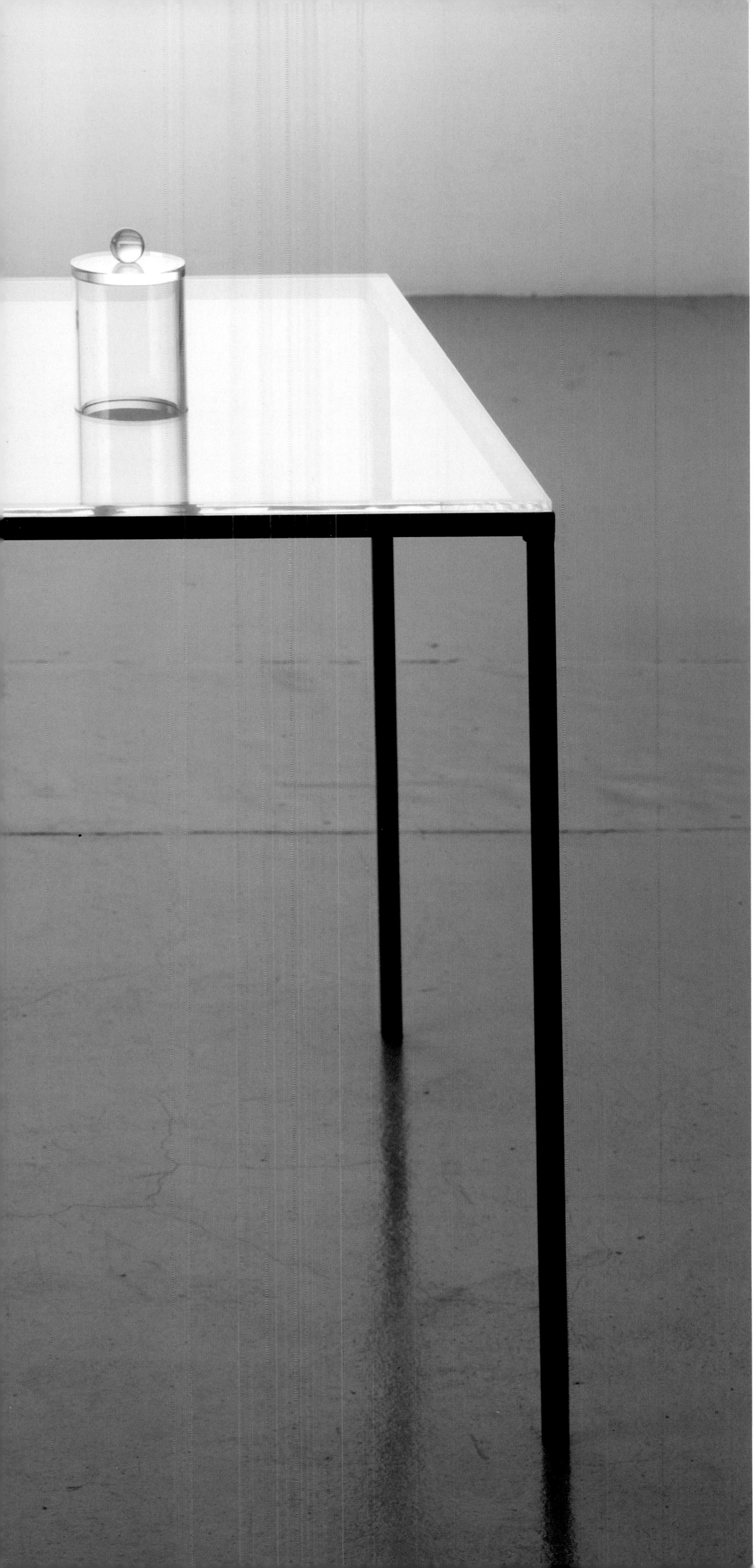

31 TABLE, 1990

OH! CHARLEY, CHARLEY, CHARLEY..., 1992

33

BOY, 1992

FAMILY ROMANCE, 1993

FIRETRUCK, 1993

CHARLES RAY

28. 8. – 9. 10. 1994    28. 8. – 23. 10. 1994

KUNSTHALLEN BERN·ZÜRICH

FASHIONS, 1996

# CHARLES RAY

Organized by
Paul Schimmel

Essays by
Paul Schimmel and Lisa Phillips

The Museum of Contemporary Art, Los Angeles
Scalo Zurich-Berlin-New York

This publication accompanies the exhibition
CHARLES RAY
organized by Paul Schimmel

and presented at
Whitney Museum of American Art, New York
June 4, 1998–August 30, 1998

The Museum of Contemporary Art, Los Angeles
November 15, 1998–March 14, 1999

Museum of Contemporary Art, Chicago
June 19, 1999–September 12, 1999


CHARLES RAY
was organized by The Museum of Contemporary Art, Los Angeles.

This exhibition is made possible by generous gifts
from Peter and Eileen Norton and the Peter Norton Family Foundation,
Lannan Foundation,
and The Eli Broad Family Foundation.

# Director's Foreword

Charles Ray is an uncanny thinker and communicator. Here we see, as one rarely does in any generation, an artist whose work in every chosen medium— photography, sculpture, performance, and film—and stylistic idiom—from the figurative to the abstract— results not only in a consistently fearless expression of his own inner convictions, but in powerful resonances with a much larger world.

This extraordinarily original artist first came to our attention nearly a decade ago when The Museum of Contemporary Art acquired **Bath**, just months after its completion in 1989, for the permanent collection. The respect that we had then for him has only grown since—aided by his presence in such landmark shows as "Helter Skelter: L.A. Art in the 1990s," and by further additions to our in-depth representation of his oeuvre in our permanent collection through the great generosity of Lannan Foundation. The latter represent Ray's finest output from many periods, including **All My Clothes** (1973), **How a Table Works** (1986), **Rotating Circle** (1988), **Tabletop** (1989), and **No** (1991).

Now, with this mid-career survey of his prolific output organized by Chief Curator Paul Schimmel, MOCA pays tribute to an artist who has in just a few years helped define, on an international scale, the role of contemporary art in the 1990s and beyond. In this time of ravenous consumerism, worship of the cult of celebrity, and questions of meaning and authenticity, Ray's work—immaculately crafted and strangely beautiful—has the rare power to be both artistically valid and culturally on the mark. It is this ability to stimulate individualistic responses, coupled with references to the culture and society of our time, that extend Ray's influence beyond its own finite disciplines and venues and make him a leading influence in contemporary art.

This comprehensive exhibition of Ray's work, documenting his career from 1973 to the present, is a tribute to the commitment and encouragement provided by Paul Schimmel for many years.Starting with the artist's first one-person exhibition in 1989 at the Newport Harbor Art Museum, Paul has, more than any other American curator, been aware of the enormous importance and potential influence of Ray's work, and has unhesitatingly followed its evolution. To Paul we owe our gratitude for this visionary involvement.

No artist's development is complete without the similarly visionary involvement of collectors who have unwavering conviction, and in this respect we laud the early and staunch commitment of Eileen and Peter Norton, Lannan Foundation and Eli Broad to Ray's work.

And lastly, of course, we express our great respect and gratitude to the artist himself. In working closely with MOCA on every phase of this major exhibition and its accompanying publication, Ray has helped fulfill the museum's purpose: to continually confront, head on, the most relevant and provocative artistic ideas of our time and share them with a large and responsive public.

Richard Koshalek
Director, The Museum of Contemporary Art

53

# Introduction and Acknowledgements

Charles Ray was included in The Museum of Contemporary Art's "Helter Skelter: L.A. Art in the 1990s" exhibition. By the time it closed, it was clear that Ray, already well-known regionally, was an artist whose reputation would be changing rapidly in the coming years. His representation focused on the figurative work that would place him squarely at the heart of the movement towards psychologically charged, body-oriented work that has characterized an overall shift in the content of art on the 1990s. His work made it clear that he was an artist of extraordinary vision, technical prowess, and emotional resonance, and it was at that time that the museum suggested a comprehensive exhibition of his work. I am deeply grateful to Charley Ray for his commitment to making this exhibition the most significant of his career.I have now had the privilege of working with Ray for over a decade, since the Newport Harbor Art Museum acquired the first of two works — Ink Box (1986) — for its permanent collection. That acquisition was precipitated by a generous gift from Edward Broida, who had become a major supporter of the work early on through the tireless enthusiasm and significant representation that Ray had received from the Los Angeles dealer, Burnett Miller. Lucinda Barnes, in addition to organizing for the Newport Harbor Art Museum the first survey of Ray's work, was singularly responsible for the acquisition of Ray' s first figurative work, Self Portrait (1990). Since Chris Burden introduced Charley' s work to me in the late 1980s, Charley has become a dear friend with whom I have traveled and sailed, and

who has never come over to my house without bringing a wonderful gift for my children (including the firetrucks that were among the models for his most significant civic sculpture). Over the years I've come to know well not only Charley, but also his friends and immediate family, including Jennifer Pastor since the late 1980s. I appreciate her friendship, and her willingness in supporting me in this project. This significant level of access is all the more remarkable given how private Ray is in his personal life. It is an acknowledgment of the importance this project has had for him that Ray has not only allowed but encouraged such intimacies. On behalf of Charley, I would also like to acknowledge his studio assistants, Manuel Alvarez, Liz Craft, and Ruby Neri.

Prior to my arrival at The Museum of Contemporary Art, Richard Koshalek, Director, acquired the first of ten works by Ray now in MOCA's permanent collection. At that time, MOCA had received a significant grant from the El Paso Natural Gas Company, for which the entire curatorial staff was responsible for recommending acquisitions. Koshalek's sole recommendation for that fund was the acquisition of Ray's work, which thus entered MOCA's collection in an early and timely fashion. His early enthusiasm continued with Ray's contribution to the "Helter Skelter" exhibition, and it was with his support that a commitment was made some six years ago for Ray to receive a major survey with a national tour organized by The Museum of Contemporary Art. Kathleen S. Bartels, Assistant Director, has assisted both in the administrative, touring, and public relations aspects of the exhibition, for which I am grateful. Erica Clark, Director of Development, coordinated the efforts to develop the necessary funds to support such an undertaking, and Jack Wiant, Chief Financial Officer, has worked closely in the development of an appropriate budget. My thanks to Dawn Setzer, former Assistant Director of Communications, Media Relations, for her hard work in handling the press related matters for the exhibition. John Bowsher and his staff made great efforts in the remaking of works, developing procedures for handling and installation, and have been instrumental in all aspects of installation for MOCA, the Whitney, and the Museum of Contemporary Art, Chicago. Robert Hollister, Registrar, and Liz Pryor, Assistant Registrar, have done a professional job in registrarial and conservation issues. Working with Tracy Bartley of the Getty Conservation Institute, they have developed a plan not only for safe transportation, but also for the continued maintenance of works that are both delicate and precise. A special thanks is for Diane Aldrich, my assistant, who in her deft and supportive manner has kept Charley informed, me on track, and has provided specific support in the development of the checklist and the tour. We have more recently been assisted by Susan Jenkins, who has brought her exceptional skills as an art historian and exhibition coordinator to this project.

This catalogue, the most comprehensive to date, has been conceived of as a collaboration between the artist, the museum, and the designer Lorraine Wild. Working with her assistant, Amanda Washburn, Lorraine has brought her great sensitivity to bear on creating an exquisitely conceived and designed catalogue. Russell Ferguson, Editor and Associate Curator, with whom I've had the pleasure of working on numerous publications over the past six years, has done a thorough and sensitive job on this publication, which will be the last that I have an opportunity to work with him on in his position as Editor. Now that his responsibilities are going to be curatorial, unfortunately, I have not found a way to c one him to continue to have his fine guidance and steady hand with the publications. I am, however, very fortunate that he has co-edited this catalogue with Stephanie Emerson, who increasingly has taken on greater responsibility in the overall publications program, and has had a significant and steadying influence on the development of this publication. I am also grateful for the tireless efforts and diligent assistance of Jane Hyun, Editorial Secretary. John Alan Farmer used his formidable skills to sensitively and intelligently edit my catalogue essay, for which I am grateful.

Throughout the years, Ray has developed a series of personal and special relationships with a number of dealers who have had to share him with each other, and support the highly limited output of his artistic activity. Hudson at Feature, New York, has been his most longstanding dealer. It is a credit both to Ray's loyalty and Hudson's understanding of the work that it has been such a long-lasting and productive relationship. In the 1990s, Ray has developed a number of very significant relationships with dealers, none more important than that with Regen Projects here in Los Angeles. Shaun Caley and Stuart Regen have been more than dealers, they have been Ray's close friends and they have had a singular impact on the creation of his most important new work, **Unpainted Sculpture** (1997). In Europe, Claudio Guenzani in Milan, and Cornelia Grassi in Milan, and then London, have made deep commitments both to him and to his work. Donald Young in Seattle, has also been a longstanding representative for Ray's work, as has Jeffrey Deitch, in New York. Deitch facilitated the work's entrance into several important collections.

Of great importance to Ray's visibility in Europe was the retrospective organized by Lars Nittve, then Director of the Rooseum, Mälmo, which traveled to London, Bern, and Zurich. I especially appreciate that when Lars approached MOCA in 1994 about participating in his Ray survey, he was understanding that we wanted to wait and organize an independent exhibition in the future for the United States. His fine exhibition and catalogue have been a valuable resource in putting together this exhibition, and gave us the opportunity to rephotograph many works in a consistent manner, which was done by Reto Pedrini of Foto-Studio H. Humm. In Los Angeles, Florence Tsang did superb photo re-touching.

This exhibition has been made possible through the extraordinary generosity of a handful of lenders who know the perils and tribulations of lending such delicate works. The importance of this exhibition is reflected in the uniform willingness of the lenders to participate, and their genuine enthusiasm. I am grateful to the following collectors, foundations, galleries and museums for their generosity: Mandy and Clifford Einstein, Dakis Joannou, Eileen and Peter Norton, Rubell Family Collections, Florence and Philippe Segalot, United Yarn Products, Inc., The Eli Broad Family

Foundation, Re Rebaudengo Sandretto Collection, Brian D. Butler, Feature Gallery, Inc., Gagosian Gallery, Galerie Hauser and Wirth, Cornelia Grassi, Marc Jancou, Orange County Museum of Art, Walker Art Center, and the Whitney Museum of American Art.

More than just a venue for the Ray exhibition, the Whitney Museum of American Art has been a partner in the realization of my long held desire to organize this exhibition. The exhibition will premiere at the Whitney, and it is appropriate given their enthusiasm towards this project from its inception and their longstanding commitment to Ray, having included him in four Biennials (in 1989, 1993, 1995, 1997). The Whitney was instrumental in bringing national attention to Ray's work. They have also exercised a lasting commitment through the acquisition of two seminal works, **Boy** (1992) and **Puzzle Bottle** (1995). I am very grateful for the enthusiasm that David Ross, Director, brought to this proposal made by Lisa Phillips, Curator, to add this show to their schedule. One could ask for no better or thoughtful a colleague to work with than Lisa Phillips, whose interest in Ray goes back to her inclusion of his work in the 1989 Whitney Biennial, and who has been a champion from that time on. I am not only grateful for her participation in this exhibition, but also for the significant contribution she has made to Ray's scholarship through her contribution to the catalogue.

In addition to the Whitney, the Museum of Contemporary Art in Chicago has provided the third and in some ways the most personal venue for the tour. Charley, having grown up in Chicago with his grandmother's art school just blocks from the MCA, made the MCA a desirable and appropriate venue for this exhibition. Kevin Consey, former Director, and

# Acknowledgements

Richard Francis, former Chief Curator, provided the initial enthusiasm for the MCA's participation in the show. I am fortunate that the acting Chief Curator, Amada Cruz, with the encouragement of Lucinca Barnes, former Curator of the permanent collection, picked up the ball through a period of change and ensured that this exhibition would have a venue in the community in which Ray grew up and where his art developed.

The Lannan Foundation has had a longstanding commitment to Charles Ray. The largest collection of his work was assembled by the foundation under the guidance of Lisa Lyons, and The Museum of Contemporary Art is fortunate today to have the most important single collection of Ray's work in large part through the Foundation's gift to the museum. Lannan Foundation supported his first survey exhibition at the Newport Harbor Art Museum, and has also, under the guidance of its Director of Art Programs, Kathleen Merrill, supported this larger-scale, traveling survey exhibition. The leadership of the Foundation and the support of J. Patrick Lannan has helped to bring wider international attention to Ray's work, and has had an indelible mark upon his career. The Eli Broad Family Foundation, in addition to their generous loan of works to the exhibition, has made a substantial contribution to the show's organization through sign ficant support toward consolidation and shipping expenses.

This exhibition could not have happened without the genuine enthusiasm for and support of its organization here at The Museum of Contemporary Art and at the Whitney Museum of American Art by Peter and Eileen Norton and the Norton Family Foundation. Ray's work has been at the center of the Norton's private collection, including works that have been promised to MOCA (Fall '91, 1992), and donated to The Museum of Modern Art (Family Romance, 1993). The Nortons's have given substantial financial assistance for the exhibition's organization and tour and I greatly appreciate their support of this project.

Paul Schimmel

# BESIDE ONE'S SELF

Paul Schimmel

It was 5:30 a.m. on a freezing, rainy morning in February when, at Charles Ray's insistence, we departed from Chicago for Marmion Military Academy in Aurora, Illinois. The years Ray spent at this military high school administered by the Benedictine order of the Catholic church constituted a period of intense and unsettling anxiety that would have a formative effect on his subsequent artistic career. The visit today was the first stop on a daylong tour of important sites from his youth that Ray had arranged for us. By the end of the day I was supposed to have a fuller knowledge of his background that would enrich my understanding of his art, in preparation for the retrospective of his work that I was organizing.

We had to leave as early as we did, Ray explained, in order to witness the students waking up at the same ungodly hour at which he had awoken day after day when he was a student. So in the darkness of predawn, we headed to the rural community just two exits south of Joliet Prison to walk the hallowed halls that had so traumatized the young adolescent. Arriving at the break of dawn, Ray felt a palpable sense of disappointment when he discovered that the rigors of early morning military marching had been supplanted by a more comforting routine. This revelation initiated a mantra he repeated throughout the morning that "things just aren't the way they used to be." Wandering the catacombs beneath the school in search of the arsenal, Ray was also surprised to learn that the students no longer used real weapons, as they had when he was a student. Instead, they now carried crudely sculpted and painted replicas. In addition, he also learned that while drilling and marching were still important components of the curriculum, they no longer occurred on a daily basis. In fact, the entire visit was ultimately dominated by an unsettling chasm between reality and what Ray had remembered and imagined.

The gap between the real and the unreal, often indistinguishable at a glance and often unsettling when one becomes aware of it, which we experienced that bitterly cold morning, is central to the concerns that Ray has explored in his art from the early 1970s to the present. Over the years Ray has often spoken of an art that can jerk one's head around—of making objects and creating situations that are not what they appear to be and that force us to re-examine the validity of the truths we garner from perceptual experience. Ray takes the bedrock of reality, whether something as abstract as a cube or as concrete as a human figure, and then twists, tweaks, and jerks it until it tugs at the reality of what one thinks one knows. In so doing, Ray unsettles the viewer's very state of being, for he shows that perception reveals reality to be not immutable but in a constant state of flux. The day's tour was supposed to confirm the realities of Ray's memories, for example, but instead forced him to confront the highly fluctuating and temporal nature of the reality on which he had based so much of his art. For me, this experience sculpted into relief both the life-like nature of Ray's art and the art-like nature of his life.

Throughout the morning, Ray's teachers recounted stories of his mischievous pranksterism. Even though he was slight in size and average in disposition, Ray was nonetheless memorable for his antics, which included marching his entire troop in drill formation down an alley into a wall. This formalized "performative sculpture," which culminated in rows of children tumbling into each other in serialized sequence, resulted from Ray's nervousness at the responsibility of leading the troop and his corresponding inability to tell his left from his right hand. Yet his conservative art teacher told me that he did not recognize Ray as a prodigy—a judgment later seconded by one of the instructors in the art school his grandmother had established and that he had also attended. When I inquired about Ray's artistic talents as a youth, this instructor proceeded to wax eloquently on the technical skills of Ray's younger brother, the real artist in the family.

To a certain extent, it seemed logical that Ray would become an artist. His family owned and operated a successful commercial art school founded by his fiercely independent grandmother, Ruth, which was later administered by his father, Wade. The school's practical, commercially-oriented curriculum and its location in the center of the city contributed to its great success. But the incongruity between the art school that Ray had known as a child and the one we visited that day was overwhelming. The original building had been sold, and the school had merged with another private institution. Although an instructor or two remembered Ray (and recounted more tales of mischievousness), the school was no longer the family business that had played such a significant role in Ray's youth.

Given his family's background in art and his own desire to enter an environment more relaxed and supportive than the one he had known in military school, it is not surprising that Ray decided to study art in college. In military school he had expressed his creativity in childlike anarchistic acts. Studying art offered him other outlets. Matriculating at the University of Iowa in Iowa City, Ray studied with the South African-born sculptor Roland Brener, who had studied in London with the renowned British sculptor Anthony Caro, whom influential critics such as Clement Greenberg and Michael Fried hailed in the 1960s as the most important modernist sculptor since David Smith. The relationship that Ray and Brener forged would become the single most critical encounter in his formative years as a sculptor. Brener provided Ray with a formal language—the high modernist sculptural syntax of Caro—that continues to inform not only how he constructs his work but how he speaks about it. In addition, Brener reinforced the young artist's passion for sailing, which, at least for Ray, is not unrelated to the activity of making sculpture. Like the formalist sculpture that Greenberg and Fried hailed in numerous influential articles and reviews in the 1960s, sailing searches for that perfect balance between stability and instability, balance and collapse. Brener taught Ray through competitive sailing how to find that line

ROLAND BRENER. TABLE TOF SCULPTURE QED, 1961.
NATIONAL GALLERY, OTTAWA

61

where the boat is perfectly balanced on the brink of disaster—a quality that Ray would explore in his earliest sculptures.[1]

While studying with Brener, Ray created a series of sculptures between 1971 and 1973 that formally investigate the tension between stability and instability by bending materials and forms to the point at which they were on the verge of literally coming unhinged. For Brener, one of the most memorable aspects of Ray's early sculpture was the sound of its making. Working with iron girders and rods, Ray's sculptural activity from this period centered on the arrangement and eventual collapse of forms that, at least for the artist, entailed more than just a visual risk. A thin, gangly teenager, Ray would drag heavy metal around the studio that Brener had so generously lent him, often at great physical danger to himself. His first self-organized exhibition, entitled "One Stop Gallery," took place in this studio.

Ray explored the formal attributes of tension, balance, and seriality in Caro's high modernist sculpture by constructing a series of situations that allowed him to experiment playfully in a semi-scientific manner. Brener, who had studied with Caro at St. Martin's School of Art in London, where he taught before coming to the University of Iowa, transmitted to Ray Caro's formal language. Nevertheless, by the early 1970s Caro was considered all but irrelevant by the most radical sculptors in the United States—the Minimalists and Postminimalists that Fried had criticized so eloquently in his seminal article "Art and Objecthood" (1967) and other writings.

Even the young British sculptors of Ray's generation such as Tony Cragg and Richard Deacon, ultimately moved away from Caro's influence to develop a new British sculpture not based on the purity of self-referential abstraction. Indeed, the entire generation of British sculptors that emerged during the early 1980s, including as well Anish Kapoor, Anthony Gormley, and Bill Woodrow, were to achieve independence through their investigation of international tendencies, most notably U.S. Minimalism and Postminimalism. But Ray, whose period of maturation was longer than that of his British counterparts, approached Caro not as a tyrant to be overthrown but as an unfamiliar figure who embodied

1 In The Optical Unconscious (Cambridge, Mass.: The MIT Press, 1993), Rosalind Krauss cites another example of the links between high modernist art and athletic activity: "We were speaking about Frank Stella and Michael asked me, 'Do you know who Frank thinks is the greatest living American?' Of course I didn't. 'Ted Williams.' And Michael Fried covered my silence with his own glee. 'Ted Williams sees faster than any other living human. He sees so fast that when the ball comes over the plate—90 miles an hour—he can see the stitches. So he hits the ball right out of the park. That's why Frank thinks he's a genius.' This was by way, of course, of inducting me onto the team, Michael's team, Frank's team, Greenberg's team, major players in the '60s formulation of modernism" (7).

INSTALLATION VIEW, ONE-STOP GALLERY, IOWA CITY, IOWA, 1971

UNTITLED, 1971

UNTITLED, 1973

UNTITLED, 1973

Brener's romantic belief in the continuing potency of formalist ideology. Even today both Brener and Ray speak reverentially of the Caroesque notion of joining the elements of a sculpture according to a formal syntax.

The most Caroesque of Ray's early sculptures is Untitled (1971). The manner in which this work sits on the floor, as well as its cherry-red finish, distinguish it as an unmistakable homage to Caro's sculpture of the 1960s. In another 1971 sculpture constructed of cement blocks and metal bars, Ray created a playful repetition of forms whose balance of tensions harks back to the reclining figures of another British modernist sculptor, Henry Moore. In his stacked tension sculptures, Ray was seeking to create a dynamic tension not only in the works themselves but also in their relationship to the viewer. He transformed the unsettling sense of tipping over, metaphorically present in Caro's work, into an object-oriented performative experience in which the viewer, by seeing the work potentially fall apart, would share the same experience that the artist himself had had—a crucial dimension of the work's "presentness."[2]

Through the elimination of welds and bolts, Ray was transforming Caro's static formal language, in which the elements of a sculpture were composed according to a syntax, into an intensely theatrical activity riven with theatricality—with the very properties of Minimalism that Fried had criticized so strongly. So theatrical was this sculpture that Ray allowed interested friends and colleagues watch him as he worked—a relief from the intensely solitary periods he often spent in the studio, which extended the loneliness and isolation he had felt in high school.[3] In Untitled (1973), for example, Ray dropped a wrecker's ball onto a sheet of metal; the resulting bends and folds of the sculpture were the result of a dramatic, even sensationalistic, process. Similarly, in another untitled sculpture of the same year, Ray dropped a plate of steel onto a neatly arranged row of fluorescent tubes. These process-oriented works demonstrate Ray's knowledge of and appreciation for Postminimalist sculptors such as Barry Le Va, who produced sculptures by shattering sheets of glass, Richard Serra, who introduced the dimension of temporality into sculpture in works such as Casting (1969) and in the related three-minute film Hand Catching Lead of the same year, and the Minimalist light work of Dan Flavin.

2 Joan Hugo, "Between Object and Persona: The Sculpture Events of Charles Ray," High Performance 8 no. 2 (issue 30) (1985): 27.
3 Ibid., 27.

One of Ray's more beautiful and prophetic pieces from this period is another untitled sculpture from 1973 in which he stacked fifteen bricks above a sawhorse and six beneath it, with the bricks held together by a heavy rope. This precariously balanced sculpture introduced into Ray's oeuvre a form that he would investigate both formally and metaphorically again and again: the plane that creates a division between above and below. The simplicity and clarity of this sculpture makes it an especially important work—certainly as important as the more well-known performative sculptures he made the same year. Increasingly, Ray was to believe that sculpture was more than an object: it was an activity.

Ray's move to the use of his own body as a sculptural element was a natural progression from this belief. He began to believe with great conviction that sculpture was an intrinsically physical activity that needed to take place every day and that was connected with notions of self-reliance, as well as with athletic activities such as rock climbing and sailing. Adopting an engineering-like aesthetic that incorporated gravity, weight, and balance as sculptural elements, Ray began a series of works centered on his own body. His most well-known works from this period are photographs showing him hanging from a diagonally positioned plank, suspended by the joint connecting his pelvis to his torso or his calves to his thighs. Dressed in a sweatshirt, jeans, and hiking boots, Ray hangs limply from the wedge between the plank and the wall. By inserting his own body into the work, he created an empathy with the viewer that extends beyond the formalistic concerns that Serra had explored in his prop pieces, such as One-Ton Prop (House of Cards) (1969). This work also suggests the influence of Bruce Nauman's videotapes of the late 1960s, such as Wall-Floor Positions (1968), in which the artist used the surfaces of walls, floors, and corners as formal structures against which to press and bounce his body.

In yet another untitled work from 1973, Ray suspended a one-ton cement block from the side of a seemingly branchless tree trunk in such a casual manner that the eye was tricked into questioning whether a trunk of that size could hold such a block and whether the block and the tree were real. The rope, tied diagonally up into the tree to provide a cantilever support for the block, created a

UNTITLED, 1973

PLANK PIECE, 1973, 1989. THE MUSEUM OF CONTEMPORARY ART, LOS ANGELES
GIFT OF LANNAN FOUNDATION, 97.89A.B

diagonal thrust that was a compositional element Ray used in most of his tension-based sculptural investigations. In a related untitled work from the same year, Ray had his own body tied up into a tree, where he remained for an afternoon. He was tied as close to a branch as possible so that passers-by would not see him at first glance, so that he would come into vision as the result of a double-take, as it were, in which the viewer questioned the reality he or she saw. In subsequent works Ray continued to pursue this attempt to blend sculpture as seamlessly as possible into its site so that the viewer would encounter it unexpectedly and then be consumed with such doubt.

These investigations reflect the influence in particular of Dennis Oppenheim, whose Parallel Series (1970) was an activity in which he tested the capacity of his body to suspend itself between two masonry walls. The stress between the walls was indexed by the position of Oppenheim's body as it arced; the artist duplicated this arc in an abandoned sump by assuming the parallel position.[4] Oppenheim's work, like that of the Viennese artist Valie Export of the same period, provided a resource for the more formal interests for which Ray had already shown a proclivity.

In an untitled performative sculpture from 1974, Ray and a female friend sat back-to-back and end-to-end on an eight-foot-long plank, suspended by their legs and held by the tension between their thighs and their calves. This poetic work echoes Constantin Brancusi's famous stone sculpture The Kiss (1907), in which two figures are joined into one block. However, in Ray's psychological counterpart, he separated the two protagonists by the large stretch of a magically suspended plank. Regarding his performative sculptures of this period, Ray would later state, "When I was putting the sculpture together I was always there, lifting and moving and sliding things, and it became really easy for me to insert myself into the work as a material. But I had never just used myself."

Ray's shift from the activity of making sculptural objects to making "sculpture that is like "behavior" coincided with his growing interest in film and serial photography. He used the four hundred dollars he received from selling poster-sized blow-ups of his untitled tree and plank suspensions to restructure backwards,

CONSTANTIN BRANCUSI
THE KISS, c 1912.
PHILADELPHIA MUSEUM OF ART:
THE LOUISE AND WALTER ARENSBERG
COLLECTION, 1950

4 See Dennis Oppenheim Selected Works, 1967–90: And the Mind Grew Fingers, exh. cat. (New York: P.S. 1 Museum, Institute of Contemporary Art and Harry N. Abrams, 1992), 48.

UNTITLED, 1973. THE MUSEUM OF CONTEMPORARY ART, LOS ANGELES
GIFT OF LANNAN FOUNDATION

UNTITLED, 1974

cut by cut, Orson Welles's classic film Touch of Evil (1958). Franklin Miller, a structural film maker teaching at the University of Iowa while Ray was a student there, as well as the multimedia and performance artist Hans Breder, encouraged the young artist to explore sculpture through these time-based mediums.

These investigations led directly to Ray's autobiographically informed photographic sequence All My Clothes (1973). Directly inspired by Eleanor Antin's Carving: A Traditional Sculpture (1972), in which she documented her weight loss through a sequence of 148 black- and-white photographs, All My Clothes is a series of sequential photographs in which Ray modeled his entire wardrobe. The sequence begins with Ray wearing his warmest outfits and ends with him modeling his shorts and a tee-shirt. With more humor, this work also evokes Howard Fried's less-known All My Dirty Blue Clothes (1969), in which the artist arranged his clothes in an eighty-foot-long chain.

Ray also produced other photographic works during this period. In an homage to yet another British sculptor, Richard Long, he took hikes and photographed his tracks. In addition, he recorded the transformation of a new white suit, socks, and shoes into black through a sequence of photographs taken over a period of days. But perhaps of greater interest is a series of photographs that Ray took under the influence of various drugs—a precedent for his later work Yes (1990). While under the influence of marijuana, LSD, and mescaline, Ray took a series of photographs that recorded his different states of consciousness. This investigation into his psychological states anticipated his psychologically charged figurative work of the 1990s.

Ray's undergraduate years were interrupted by a move to Vancouver, where he continued his studies informally with Brener. However, with the exception of a brief spurt of creativity, this period proved to be relatively unproductive. In 1975 Ray graduated from the University of Iowa after returning from his one-year hiatus in Vancouver. Upon graduation he returned to his parents' home in Chicago for a year. He then began graduate school at the University of Kentucky in Lexington, where he studied with visiting artist Siah Armajani and Derrick Woodham. After a period in which he struggled with the decision of whether

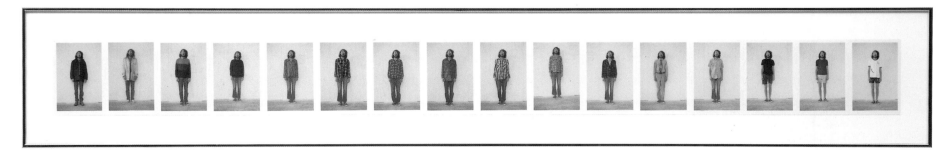

ALL MY CLOTHES, 1973
THE MUSEUM OF CONTEMPORARY ART, LOS ANGELES
GIFT OF LANNAN FOUNDATION

UNTITLED, 1976

to pursue performance or sculpture, in which he was "just floating, drifting," as he has remarked, Ray began to work with a material whose transparency entranced him: glass. He proceeded to create an important series of glass works that focused on the visually disorienting qualities of this material in order to disrupt the perceived stability of dimensional reality.

Ray created this series of distinctive glass works in 1975 and 1976. Untitled (1976) was a bed encased in a glass vitrine, on top of which lay a pillow. This sculpture was the first of what would become his lifelong exploration of the visually and psychologically disorienting effects of objects above and below planar surfaces, in which he attempted to deconstruct the opposition between these two terms. However, Armajani told Ray at the time that the work was too complicated and trite. In a second glass work Ray replaced an iron railroad tie embedded in the train tracks with a hollow glass one of exactly the same dimensions. When a train rolled over the tracks, spectators were surprised that it did not break. Finally, the most sculptural of all of Ray's glass works was Untitled (Glass Chair) (1976). For this work he sliced the legs of an old-fashioned wooden chair, designed for a school teacher, seven inches above the floor with a six-by-six-foot sheet of glass. The glass created a reflective, mirror-like surface that disoriented the viewer by confounding one's perception of where the chair ended and where its reflection began. This disruptive visual device was protean enough to be deployed in several subsequent works.

But Ray's favorite glass work—and the one Armajani most emphatically supported—was an installation in which glass plates, cut into the exact shape of the steps on a staircase, were suspended seven inches above the actual steps. The sheets of glass both defined and defiled the function of the staircase, creating in the viewer a disorienting sense of vertigo that made one feel as if one might tumble down. The icy, dreamlike quality of this work starkly contrasted with the very real possibility of falling and shattering the glass—a rich metaphor for the instability of perceptual experience and the reality it constructs.

After studying at the University of Kentucky, Ray transferred to the Mason Gross School of Art at Rutgers University in New Brunswick, New Jersey, where

UNTITLED (GLASS CHAIR), 1976
COLLECTION FLORENCE AND PHILIPPE SEGALOT

he finally received his M.F.A. in 1979. In 1978 Ray created the first of a series of sculptures based on the structure of the cube—In Memory of Moro, a title that refers to Aldo Moro, a prominent Italian politician affiliated with the Christian Democratic party who was kidnaped and executed by the terrorist organization the Red Brigade in 1978. In this sculpture Ray aggressively, yet humorously, confronted the powerful legacy of Minimalism. The quintessential Minimalist structure was perhaps the cube; Tony Smith, Donald Judd, and Richard Serra are among the most well-known Minimalist and Postminimalist sculptors who investigated this structure. Although In Memory of Moro is in the form of a hollow cube, Ray poked a hole through the top of the structure, from which emerged his arm holding a red flag. The sculpture is simultaneously a memorial for a highly charged political situation, as well as a critique of the relationship of power constructed between certain Minimalist sculptures and the viewer, such as Smith's Die (1962), for example, a black cube the size of a human being with a decidedly aggressive title.

That same year Ray created Clock Man, another work activated by his own body. He replaced a public clock with a clock similar in scale and location but with one distinctive difference: Ray's legs hung where the clock's pendulum normally did. Ray attempted to keep time based on his own internal sense of duration rather than on official chronometric measurement; when the performance concluded at 3 p.m., Ray thought it was 6:00 p.m. In both In Memory of Moro and Clock Man Ray used his body in an increasingly surrealist rather than formalist manner. No longer was his body a device used to explore the effects of gravity and geometry. Instead, his seemingly dismembered limbs animated sculptures in a visually and psychologically unsettling way. Like Surrealist artists such as René Magritte, who have proven to be significant for Ray's sculptural activities of the 1990s, these works transformed disjunctive elements—a cube and an arm, a clock and two legs—into a hallucinogenically disruptive metaphor.

By the end of the 1970s, after Ray had finally finished his graduate studies, he produced a series of more formal academic works consisting of sculptures of dogs realized in a geometric, highly stylized manner. By 1981, when he began

72

IN MEMORY OF MORO, 1978

CLOCK MAN, 1978

teaching at the University of California in Los Angeles at the invitation of Ray Brown, who was then the chair of the Department of Fine Arts, he had reached a formal dead end. His confidence and morale were at an all-time low, and his sense of professional despair was exacerbated by a tragic personal crisis: the death of his younger brother Aaron from lymphoma. This event motivated Ray to make a memorial to Aaron. No longer willing to create sculptural toys, as the dog sculptures had become, Ray once again turned to his own body to transform and reinvigorate his sculptural ambitions.

In Memory of Sadat (1981) is a coffin-like tomb bisected down the middle, in which Ray's arm from the elbow up and his leg from the knee down disorientingly protruded from the sculpture's rough steel exterior; these bodily fragments almost resembled hieroglyphs whose meanings were inscrutable to the untutored viewer. The split in the rectangular, pedestal-like form allowed a small crack of light to penetrate the structure, though it was not strong enough for the viewer to see the body within. The split also emphasized the separateness of the arm and the leg, effectively and disturbingly dividing the body in two. Although Ray began the sculpture as a personal memorial to his brother, the title suggests a broader political dimension. It refers to Anwar Sadat, the president of Egypt who had signed a historic peace treaty with Israel in 1979 and was assassinated in 1981. Like In Memory of Moro, this work is a cool, Postminimalist monument to a political cause in which the artist had no deep and abiding interest.

In a related untitled work from 1981 to 1985, Ray used the same form of a limb protruding from a steel plate but allowed the weight of the plate to rest directly on his body. Until that time he had used his limbs to activate his Post-minimalist sculptures in a specifically iconographic manner. With this work, he reversed the relationship, and the formal plate activated the body sculpturally rather than vice versa. Ray was becoming increasingly conscious of how to manipulate the tension between the plane and what lay both beneath and above it.

A case in point is Shelf (1981), which anticipated several aspects of Ray's subsequent work. For this sculpture Ray positioned a shelf on a wall at neck level, on which he then placed three gray still-life objects, along with his head, which

74

SHELF, 1981

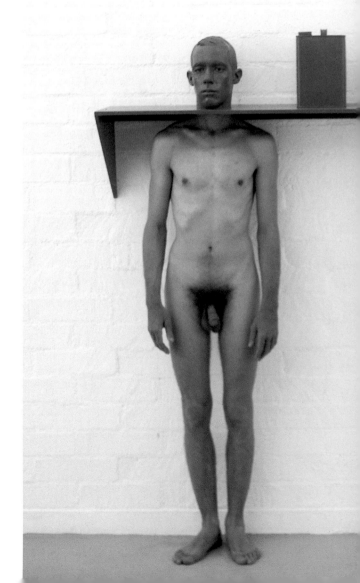

was similarly colored. Below the gray still lifes Ray's own body, posed in an aggressive stance of full frontal nudity, was visible. The work is disconcerting because his head, which seemed to have been transformed into an inanimate object, appeared to have been separated from his living body. The viewer was both attracted by the frozen quality of Ray's head and fearful of the soul embedded within it, which was virtually unreadable. This early performative sculpture provided a clear avenue for future investigations, such as Male Mannequin (1990), in which Ray fitted a generic mannequin with a cast of his own genitals.

In 1983 Ray, who had been unsuccessful in securing a venue for these difficult-to-show and difficult-to-sell sculptures, rented the former studio of the artist Robert Graham, located in a visible part of Venice, California. He installed In Memory of Moro, In Memory of Sadat, and Untitled in separate rooms and performed the sculptures from 1 p.m. to 5 p.m. every half hour, four days a week for two weeks. The controlled and progressive nature of this installation is characteristic of how Ray subsequently exhibited his static sculptural work at the Los Angeles Institute of Contemporary Art (LAICA) in 1984 and New Langton Arts in San Francisco in 1985. By isolating the works from each other and by creating highly staged and theatrical situations for viewing them, he allowed the viewer to experience each work on a one-to-one basis.

Just as Ray's self-organized exhibition in his teacher's studio in 1971 led to greater recognition and attention, so did this self-organized exhibition of 1983. However, the results were not what Ray might have imagined. Attempting to escape the necessity of performing his sculptures himself, two years later Ray hired models so that the works could be seen simultaneously and without his direct involvement. The result, however, was an unmitigated disaster, and Ray began to reconsider his commitment to participating to such a high degree in the exhibition of his sculptures. Works like The Examination (1984) and At the Table (1984), while furthering Ray's interests in creating sculptural situations that were formally activated by his own body, also exacerbated the exhaustion of having to perform his work himself.

By 1985, when he was being interviewed for a cover story in the magazine

AT THE TABLE, 1984

THE EXAMINATION, 1984

High Performance, Ray announced that "the problem right now [is] there's beginning to be interest in showing the work and I'm getting worn out . . .. Instead of dealing with the body as a persona I'd like it to integrate or implicate the spectator, so that without being participatory it would still acknowledge and manipulate them somehow. . . . I just can't do it myself anymore, maybe in five years."[5] This, of course, was never to be the case. However, Ray eventually found a means of removing himself from his work while creating sculptures that satisfied his increasingly complex demands.

The table provided the support, the ground, that would prove to be the juncture between Ray's performative sculpture and his subsequent work. Like the plane of glass or the shelf, the table provided a formal structure on which Ray could introduce figurative and still-life elements. It was a structure through which Ray could investigate the relational psychology between figures in a formal manner, and it was the platform on which he could move to the little-explored idiom of sculptural still life.

In The Examination Ray created a highly angular and structured table and chair that revealed the artist's body, with the exception of the head, which was enveloped by a circle. The angularity of this sculpture evoked Ray's years at the military academy, where he had been forced to eat a "square meal." The highly controlled structure of these social events piqued the artist's interest in visualizing the kinds of social interactions that took place on and around the table.

Another early sculpture that uses the form of the table is At the Table. This work incorporated two figures, one seated and one standing, and called Ray's attention to increasingly complex issues of social interaction. Were the figures a student and teacher or perhaps a waiter and patron? Was the situation one of dominance and submission? Ultimately, Ray chose to represent himself and another male figure so as not to emphasize the connotations suggested by a male/female interaction.

One of Ray's most important nonperformative table sculptures of this period is Viral Research (1986). Although the title of this work suggests its relationship to the public clamor surrounding the isolation of HIV, the virus that causes

77

5 Ray, in Hugo, 29.

AIDS, in 1985, it stems from the artist's much deeper and darker fascination with mortality in general, especially his own. This fascination was no doubt intensified by the death of his brother. In addition, during the period in which he made Viral Research, Ray and his wife were in the middle of a painful divorce. Lonely and isolated, Ray would walk with his dog on the beach and would collect containers washed ashore by winter storms. These objects provided the initial inspiration for what became a greatly reduced and simplified composition consisting of eight glass containers arranged on a Plexiglas table interconnected by a glass conduit. As with all of Ray's still-life works, the process of making the final selection of pitchers, bottles, jars, and glasses was painstakingly laborious. His former professor Roland Brener assisted him by encouraging him to refine his selection to far fewer elements than the sixty to seventy containers he had collected and to eliminate the more tangled web of interconnected tubes beneath the Plexiglas table top. Ray was aware of a work that Brener had made—a table in which all of the parts could be removed and fitted inside the table itself for transport. Finally, as in Untitled (Glass Chair), Viral Research uses a reflective surface to distort the reality of above and below, inside and outside, and as in Shelf and Gangrene, this use of a unifying visual feature both coheres and distorts discrete visual elements.

In How A Table Works (1986) Ray created a still life of objects arranged on a table held together by a tubular steel framework, which in many respects mimics the forms Ray had arrived at through reduction in Viral Research. Like the glass plate that sliced through the chair in Untitled (Glass Chair), the table top was a planar surface that called for exploration of the theme of illusion versus reality, a longstanding theme in the history of Western painting, especially in the genre of still life. The composition of Ray's highly theatricalized still lifes suggests a relationship with the artist Giorgio Morandi, whom Ray greatly admires. While Morandi brings order to the overall pattern and structure of the elements on the picture plane, Ray's utter destruction of the solidity of the picture plane itself undermines any notion of solidity and calmness. In fact, even though Ray chose objects with great sensitivity to their formal relationships with each other, he created a performative situation in which the very solidity of the concept of table was questioned. In a humorous reversal of Joseph Kosuth's platonic exploration of the meaning of "chair" in One and Three Chairs (1965), Ray was searching for the ideal table, which in fact exists in a transitory and fleeting state.

Three years after Ray made How a Table Works he turned to this structure again. Tabletop (1989) consists of six objects arranged on a table. At first glance the objects seem stationary. But, in fact, they rotate so slowly that without patience—the very same patience that one needs to see Minimalist paintings—the viewer would not know that they are rotating at all. When he made this sculpture, Ray had become interested in Uri Geller, an illusionist who was allegedly able to move objects with his mind. Motorizing the objects on the table allowed Ray to explore formally the properties of kinesthesia without recourse to illusionism or to mind-expanding drugs. Tabletop permitted him to explore the boundaries of peripheral vision and to create motion that readjusted the line where recognition begins. Once Ray had conceived of a table with slowly rotating objects, he struggled to find essentially circular objects that did not have strong narrative or contextual qualities. Although the simple wooden table, plastic tumbler, aluminum shaker, terra cotta pot, and plastic bowl display the Americana quality of his youth in the Midwest in the 1950s, he chose the objects primarily for their uniformly circular shapes, which made it difficult for the viewer to notice their movement.

The most recent of Ray's sculptures that incorporates a table is Table (1990). This work displays his continuing interest in the issues of transparency and inside/outside that had been the impetus for Viral Research and that had no doubt found initial manifestation in his glass works of the mid-1970s. The simplest of Ray's tables, Table is an exquisitely simple resolution of his explorations into perception, functionality, and inside/outside without tricks, pumps, inks, or motors. Instead, Ray fused the Plexiglas table top with the Plexiglas objects that stand on and are embedded into its planar surface.

In 1986, the same year in which Ray made Viral Research and How a Table Works, he also created what is arguably the most successful sculpture he had made to that date, Ink Box. This work combined with great simplicity and clarity aspects of Ray's formal training with his interest in the performative and the participatory. Returning to the form of the cube, which had served him so well in many of his performative sculptures, Ray created a black cube even more destructive of the homogeneity of form than In Memory of Moro. In Ink Box Ray produced an illusion of solidity that disguised the fact that the work was dangerously unstable: a black box with an open top filled to the brim with two hundred gallons of printer's ink, which exactly matched the texture, color, and reflectivity of the black painted sides. Not unlike his earlier performative sculptures, this work has a life of its own—a fulfillment of Ray's desire to make a sculpture that did not require his direct participation and that would still "come out of the notion of event. I'm really interested in the relationship of people to things, so the next work will probably have something to do with events and with people."[6]

In a decidedly mischievous manner, Ray implicated the viewer in the work by capitalizing on the inability of many individuals to control the natural desire to touch shiny, reflective, polished surfaces. With this work he hoped to strike at the viewer's almost neurotic urge to touch the surface, even though one knows that the cube is not solid and that the result would be disastrous. Like much performance art, myths have developed around this simple, yet highly complex, work. The stories surrounding those who have allegedly touched, splattered, and dropped objects into it have become legion. For example, the story of the elegantly dressed patron of the Newport Harbor Art Museum in Newport Beach, California, whose long strand of pearls descended into the ink as she bent over the cube, is beautifully powerful in its simplicity, however untrue the story is. Ink Box even spawned a sequel of sorts, Ink Line (1987). Focusing on the same kinesthetic desire to touch, Ray created this stream of black ink that ran like a string from the ceiling of his studio to the floor.

Another important work in which Ray used black liquid as a metaphorical reference to death is Tub with Black Dye (1986). To create this work he filled a bathtub, an object he would use again in 1988, to the brim with black dye, visible

6 Ibid.

both on the surface and through eight hundred holes plugged with stubby test tubes. In the fascistic and repetitive pattern of the nipple-like test-tube protrusions, Ray made plain his desire to articulate the interior as the subject of the exterior. These reversals of inside and outside, explored through Ray's own protruding limbs in his earlier performative sculptures, manifested themselves in this work, distinguished by its unusually complex surface. One of his personal favorites, it is in marked contrast to the second bathtub work he produced two years later. In that work, Ray rotated a bathtub ninety degrees from a horizontal (sculptural) orientation to a vertical (pictorial) one. Filled with liquid contained behind a plate of glass, he created an elegant, yet disorienting, trompe l'oeil, with none of the psychological implications of Tub with Black Dye, which he has described as a realization of his childhood love of the famous Etruscan sculpture of Romulus and Remus. However, he replaced the life-giving milk of the mother's breast with black ink connoting death.

After Ink Box and Ink Line, Ray created an even more dangerously unstable, sculptural encounter for the public. He constructed a rapidly rotating circle flush with and the same color as the surrounding floor. Spinning at hundreds of revolutions per minute, this rotating circle was visually indistinguishable from its surroundings. Ray ultimately abandoned this work in favor of Rotating Circle, a circle with the dimensions of Ray's head installed flush in a wall at head level. This circle rotates so rapidly that it appears to be stationary, so its most pronounced effect on the viewer is auditory: the hum of the motor tips off the unsuspecting passer-by that something is not as it should be. With concise means, Ray created a real event that functioned as an abstraction and an abstraction that functioned in the real world. As he had done with the Minimalist cube, he turned Robert Irwin's Zen-like, perceptually-oriented disks on end by investing these contemplatively spiritual objects with a nihilistic danger—that, again, was only perceived as the result of a double-take in which one was forced to question the truth of what one thought one saw.

Another sculpture of this period that confounds the viewer's expectations

81

of what one thinks one sees and what one really sees is 32x33x35=34x33x35 (1989), a brushed aluminum cube whose interior is deeper than the exterior, as the title indicates. This subtle but powerfully disorienting difference in depth creates a physically unsettling quality for the viewer, an effect Ray had explored success-fully in Untitled (Glass Chair), Staircase, and many of his performative works. As with Viral Research, Ray made a structure that problematized for the viewer the distinction between inside out and outside in.

But the most aggressively sculptural of all the cubes is 7½-Ton Cube (1990). In contrast to Pepto-Bismol in a Marble Box (1989), an extravagantly baroque cube that features a marble exterior and a Pepto-Bismol-filled interior, 7½-Ton Cube is simple and straightforward. Flawlessly finished in a buff white enamel, this sculpture looks much lighter than the title indicates. In yet another subversion of Minimalism, Ray encapsulated the mass of Serra in the finish fetish of John McCracken. As with the surface of its visual counterpart Ink Box, he misinforms the already suspicious viewer by telling the truth (the cube does, in fact, weigh as much as the title indicates). Goaded by the British sculptor Anthony Gormley, who claimed that Ray's work was all pumps, motors, and complex installation requirements, Ray created in 7½-Ton Cube a straightforward sculpture that nevertheless subverted the authority of perception as a route to truth.

At the same time that Ray was making his last table and cube in 1990, he introduced a new element into his repertoire of abstract, object-oriented sculptures. With Self-Portrait (1990), he shattered the general impression of his oeuvre as a formal investigation into the expanded properties of abstract sculpture. Even though Ray had previously used his body to activate his sculptures and had in some cases made the abstracted body the subject of his sculptural activity, his announcement in 1989 that he was working on a self-portrait in which he would wear his favorite sailing outfit was nonetheless shocking. On the heels of his first brush with success, Ray changed the direction of his work and chose to do something quite the opposite of his formal investigations. By moving from the generalized use of his body in sculpture to a specific representation of himself as a sculpture, Ray left himself open to charges of narcissism, vanity, and self-aggrandizement, all of which constitute the very tension that made the sculpture work. Working with commercial mannequin makers, Ray altered a standard Sears & Roebuck mannequin by adding a representation of his own head, which he had modified so that it was more generalized. With great care, he then purchased the exact outfit, from hat to shoes, that he most often wore and was most comfortable in. The resulting work was in fact a representation of Ray wearing the clothing that he most associated with one of his most pleasurable activities, sailing.

For Ray, Self-Portrait and the other figurative works that were to follow created a dramatic and consequential change in his public recognition. He began to embark on a new trajectory in which he would "sculpt" his own psyche. Ray increasingly began to step outside of himself and to examine his psyche as an object that could be manipulated. Underscoring the psychological dimension of Self-Portrait, Ray has explained that his inspiration for making the work was revenge. His once-friendly relationship with Ray Brown, the dean of the Department of Fine Arts at UCLA, who had brought him to the university, had become openly adversarial over philosophical differences about the department's future course. While visiting a department store, Ray once fantasized that by introducing Ray-ized mannequins into such stores, he could send Brown over the edge by deluding him into believing that Ray had infiltrated his consciousness to such a degree that even mannequins were beginning to look like him—a fantasy that embodied equal parts of Freudian psychology and The Twilight Zone. Ray, who had worked as a janitor at a department store during his freshman year of college, was aware of the uneasy tension between a viewer's perception of mannequins as inanimate objects and as living beings. By only slightly altering the mannequin he hoped to isolate that point of tension between the generic and the specific, the objective and the subjective, thus disorientating the viewer, who became his unwitting "victim" in place of Brown. The work thus functions by creating a gap between what is real and what is imagined. The resulting uneasiness is like the space between the floor and the bottom cube an uncomfortable nowhere land where disbelief is suspended and plausibility steps in.

Ray conceived his next mannequin figure, Male Mannequin, at about the same time that he conceived Self-Portrait. In this work, he endowed a generic mannequin with a highly realistic facsimile of his own genitals. The verisimilitude of the genitals contrasts strikingly with the genericized body of the mannequin from which they hang. Although Ray gave the mannequin an identity where there had previously been none, it still lacked life. The resulting disjunction is profoundly disconcerting.

In 1990 Ray created another self-portrait entitled Yes. He enlarged to life-size a four- by-five color transparency of his head and torso shot while he was under the influence of LSD. He then placed the resulting print in a convex frame beneath convex protective glass. Mounted on a convex wall of exactly the same angle, Yes appears to be perpendicular to the floor at first glance. One feels the bowing of the wall before one sees it, and the space seems to "marshmallow around" as if one were perceiving it under the influence of hallucinogenic drugs. It is only when one's peripheral vision brings into focus the intersection of the curved wall on which the photograph hangs with the straight walls that adjoin it that one realizes why something is not quite right. This realization provokes the queasy, unsettling feeling characteristic of Ray's works. In this respect, Ray seemed to affirm a visionary, yet dangerous, state of existence that focused on the instability of perceptual experience—a conclusion supported by the work's title.

In 1992 Ray created a counterpart to Yes entitled No. Whereas Yes pushed a subjective state outward into an objective, convex environment, No passed off an objectification of Ray as a subjective representation of the artist. Instead of using a mannequin, he had a fiberglass body mold of his head and hands fabricated and painted in a lifelike manner. Ray then photographed the body mold and presented the photograph in the same format as Yes, but in a straight frame. From a psychological standpoint No is one of Ray's most disturbing self-portraits

84

because it is so lifelike and yet so lifeless. When one looks carefully at the photograph, it resembles Ray himself, subjected to an exceedingly bad makeup job, rather than an inanimate facsimile of him. And in spite of the fact that it represents him more accurately than any of his other self-portraits, one is unable to discern from it any sense of the person within. As Ray has stated, Yes was hallucinatory, and No was delusional.

Ray's next notorious mannequin was Fall '91 (1992), which inspired a degree of international attention that he had been on the verge of receiving for the previous three years. Fall '91 is a eight-foot-tall mannequin in which every element has been enlarged by one-third. For Ray, the viewer would ideally encounter the mannequin from a distance, with no identifying features of scale in proximity, so that it would be read as of normal size. However, as one approached the mannequin, one would begin to feel increasingly smaller relative to her amazon-like stature. First exhibited in January 1992 in the group exhibition "Helter Skelter: L.A. Art in the 1990s," which I organized for The Museum of Contemporary Art in Los Angeles, Fall '91 created a sensation. Struggling to finish the work before the opening, Ray decided at the last minute to install it in a large room at the end of a long vista. This decision allowed the work to stand both visibly and metaphorically alone. Beyond its formal ability to manipulate scale and space, the work reminded the viewer of what it was to be a child again by evoking both the comfort and the fear a child has when looking up to his or her heroically-scaled parent. For many viewers, "The Big Lady," as she was informally called, became a monument to a psychologically dysfunctional maternal relationship. In fact, Ray originally conceived it as a large male figure, but, as he has stated, "I thought within a month that it should be a woman."

In Fall '91 Ray was now addressing issues of identity, gender, and sexuality, all of which were at the core of the feminist art movement of the 1970s and its second wave in the 1980s. As he had done with other movements, Ray began to enter into the disputed terrain of women's work and feminist themes. He conflated the popular culture of the fashion industry with three separately dressed, hero-

85

ically-scaled women: the "Pink Lady" with her sassy Hollywood brand of glamour, the more subtle woman in a blue suit, and the hard-driven New York working woman in her black-and-white ensemble. He pursued his interest in fashion in *The Most Beautiful Woman in the World* (1993), a series of photographs of the model Tatjana Patitz, and in *Fashions* (1996), a 16mm, 12-minute film. Ray was attracted to fashion because it was a potent metaphor for identity itself as something that can be altered, manipulated, and used to create a false intimacy between the subject and the viewer. The tension between the private photographs Ray made of Tatjana and the public images that interested him revealed the disquieting division within one person through the vehicle of the mass media, shattering the humanistic fiction that the self is whole and unified.

COVER, PARKETT, 1983

In 1992 Ray created another mannequin entitled *Boy*. For this work, he enlarged a prepubescent boy to his own size. Originally, he wanted to dress this oversized boy in a sailor's outfit, drawing on his own memories of being publicly humiliated when he was forced to wear such an outfit to a fashion show at the age of six. As Ray struggled to find an outfit to bring poignancy to the figure, he ultimately chose an infant suit altered to fit the older boy, a look which hovers between baby and Hitler youth. With *Boy*, he transformed the experience of his own awkward, uncomfortable youth into a child who radiates a powerful, evil quality; in this respect, he remakes himself from a nerd into a Damien-type figure, the juvenile incarnation of Lucifer in the popular film *The Omen*.

In *Oh! Charley, Charley, Charley . . .*(1992), Ray created his most ambitious multifigure sculpture. Drawing with chalk on the cement floor of his studio, he began this work with the intention of making a double of himself. Initially, he had conceived of a boy, himself as a youth, sitting in his own lap—an exploration of child abuse distinguished by the fact that father and son were one and the same. However, Ray then decided to produce a more ambitious work. Using eight separate body molds, he created a complex, baroque composition representing an orgy of one, in eight parts, that conflated masturbatory sexuality with Minimalist seriality. He has stated that the result was ultimately "kind of sad. . . .

I thought it would be more sexual than it was somehow." Indeed, the bloodless, lifeless, nonpenetrating sexuality of Oh! Charley, Charley, Charley . . .was to prove how flat and iconographically deadened a highly charged, sexually provocative subject could be. Ray transformed the most private of acts, masturbation, into what he regarded as a radical, contemporary, multifigure, public sculpture in the tradition of Auguste Rodin's The Burghers of Calais (1889).

Family Romance (1993) marked the end of Ray's psychologically-charged, figurative sculptures, which were increasingly becoming textbook illustrations for Freudian abnormalities. The father has gone to pot a bit, perhaps the result of having drunk too many beers; the middle-aged mother seems bored with him; but the two children appear relatively alert, with the young boy, perhaps Ray himself, looking straight out. Humorously referencing the politically correct climate in which it was made, Family Romance explored the idealism of a nuclear family in which the youngest and smallest member is treated with the same respect and importance as the traditionally dominant father. Ray brought the children halfway up in scale and the parents halfway down so that they are equal in size; none is more removed from its original scale than another. This manipulation of scale was partially inspired by a series of sculptures at Forest Lawn Cemetery in Los Angeles: a statue of a woman on a globe and a statue of a baby on a globe, produced by different artists at different times, which happened to be installed on the same scale on the same portico. While the psychological implications were relatively easy for Ray to master, the relational joining of the parts were the focus of his struggle to realize Family Romance. Distinguished by an iconic frontality, the mannequin sculptures that constitute Family Romance are arranged in a plodding, deliberate manner that mimics the structure of military school. Perhaps returning to the lessons he learned in his Caro-educated youth, Ray struggled mightily to unite the disparate elements of the sculpture through the conceit of their clasped hands. Indeed, the work focuses on the formal difficulties of juncture just as much as it does on its psychological implications. More than in any other work, this sculpture demonstrates Ray's command of Minimalist seriality.

In contrast to Oh! Charley, Charley, Charley . . . and Family Romance, whose focus was the human figure, Firetruck (1993) centered on a toy. In this sculpture a child's toy firetruck is enlarged to the scale of a real one. Produced for the 1993 Whitney Biennial, Firetruck explores the ambitions of children, which we often accept as admirable in youth and a corrupting influence in adults. It is through the ambitions of a child's imagination that this toy firetruck has grown up to be the scale of its real counterpart. So close in scale to the real thing, but so obviously different, Firetruck was parked on the street in front of the Whitney Museum of American Art during the run of the biennial. Ray hoped that on the streets of New York the sculpture would both stick out and fit in seamlessly within the urban environment. However, surrounded by a protective barrier and police protection, Firetruck stood out like a sore thumb. It was as if the theme of childlike ambition had turned on itself to become a cruel, psychological punishment for its creator. On the night of the biennial's opening Ray was transported back to a traumatic episode from his childhood, when he had brought a doll to a party where the big boys were no longer playing with little children's toys.

After the enormous push to complete Oh! Charley, Charley, Charley . . ., Family Romance, and Firetruck in 1993, Ray took the year of 1994 off in preparation for his retrospective. In spite of this respite, he produced a poster on the occasion of the exhibition for the Kunsthalle Zürich that was a loving, poetic reclaiming of the public persona he had so carefully constructed and that had been so dramatically altered since he achieved international recognition. In this poster, Ray conflated his first figurative work Self-Portrait with his real boat in a setting off the coast of California's Channel Islands. Dressing himself in a manner consistent with his first mannequin sculpture, Ray posed as identically as possible, transforming himself into the Phantom Charley that he had previously been exploring through nonperformative means.

By 1994 Ray desired to move away from figurative sculpture into abstraction, which he regards as a more moral, more honest type of art. He increasingly began to alter the human figure through a process of abstraction that often included

88

DETAIL, FIRETRUCK, 1993. THE ELI BROAD FAMILY FOUNDATION, SANTA MONICA; COURTESY GAGOSIAN GALLERY, NEW YORK AND LOS ANGELES

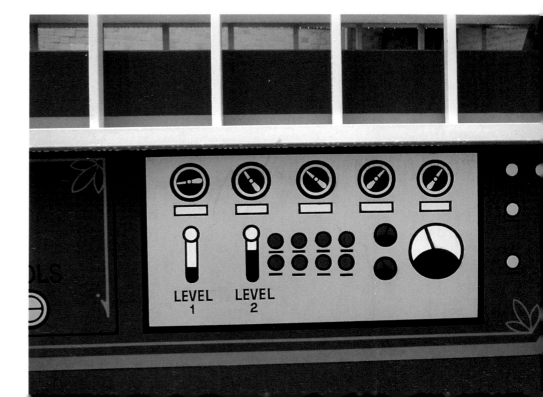

photography and film. In Puzzle Bottle (1995) Ray contained a sculpture of himself within an abstraction. "I thought if I commandeered a ship in a bottle space, it would free me up," he has stated. "The space inside the bottle could free me to make anything I wanted." Working with a craftsperson in Santa Fe, Ray created a puzzle out of his body so that its individual elements could be reconstructed inside the bottle to exacting degree. In its exploration of the ambiguity of interior and exterior, the figure in the bottle marked a return to the formal interests that had occupied Ray so consistently in his earlier sculptures. Increasingly, Ray was sculpting a pop persona that seemed completely revealing while simultaneously revealing nothing at all—an emptiness filled with a faux intimacy.

Fashions (1996), a 16mm, 12-minute film emerged directly from Ray's exploration of the formal and psychological implications of the space inside a bottle in Puzzle Bottle. Working with one of his friends, the artist Frances Stark, Ray created a short film with obvious parallels to his 1973 photographic work All My Clothes. When exhibited, the film is shown along with its projector, which evokes the film projection systems from high schools in the 1960s. The film itself shows Stark wearing a hundred different outfits selected by Ray, who transforms her into a Pop sculpture that rotates endlessly on a platform at a slow speed with an outfit change at the end of each rotation. Ray's objective was to orchestrate a non-narrative sequence of outfits that would build to nothing, with no crescendo.

Ray's most recent sculpture is Unpainted Sculpture (1997). For this work he laboriously cast in fiberglass and then reconstructed several hundred parts of a Pontiac Grand Am that had been destroyed in a cataclysmic car crash. Ray spent months visiting insurance lots to find the perfect "platonic car wreck" that avoided the narrative connotations of Edward Kienholz's and Andy Warhol's investigations of similar subjects "to transcend the subject, even though the subject always has to be there as the thing you're kicking, like one element of an equation." The resulting work solved many formal and iconographical issues that had fascinated Ray throughout his career. The model of Caro's abstraction could be found in any number of passages of twisted and compressed metal, cast in fiberglass and transformed into a gloriously shimmering abstraction of lights and darks. The life that had been lost in the fatal wreck and its ghost-like presence evoked the centrality of the body in so much of Ray's early performative sculpture. The technique of casting objects and transforming them into deadened and false representations suggested such works as Oh! Charley, Charley, Charley . . .. The sheer force of the accident had turned what was inside out and outside in, a concern evidenced in many of his earlier works. Similarly, the presence of death, another obsession, lay in the blood stains that Ray found on the inside roof of the car.

Inspired by a joke that Ray had once during a casual dinner about a student who repeatedly wrecked his roommate's car, Unpainted Sculpture began in Ray's mind as a ghost car that entombed a figure lost in a terrible and tragic accident. It evolved into an increasingly abstract sculpture treated with a soft patina of gray underpaint that was lyrically inconsistent with Ray's earlier work. Transformed into painted fiberglass, Ray's horribly crushed and disfigured car was invested with magical quality that one would never have imagined from such a grisly source. As Ray stated after a weekend of interviews with me, "I think the disturbing thing about this work is its position as reality or fantasy. It's like looking at Titanic. Is it real or computer-generated? Am I an atheist or a Catholic? Or like Oh! Charley, Charley, Charley . . ., is it a flat literary fantasy or a real disturbance in me? I think that is part of the tension, a little bit at least." The tension resulting from this inability to distinguish the real from the unreal, from the inability to discern the truth that lies behind the veneer of perceptual experience, has been present in Ray's life-like art and his art-like since his youth, as I learned on that cold day in February, searching with Ray for a truth that was basically no more than artful invention.

90

DETAILS, UNPAINTED SCULPTURE, 1997.
WALKER ART CENTER, MINNEAPOLIS; GIFT OF BRUCE AND MARTHA ATWATER, ANN AND BARRIE BIRKS, DOLLY FITERMAN,
ERIN AND MIRIAM KELEN, LARRY PERLMAN AND LINDA PETERSON PERLMAN, HARRIET AND EDSON SPENCER
WITH ADDITIONAL FUNDS FROM THE T.B. WALKER ACQUISITION FUND, 1998

# CHARLES RAY: Castaway

## Lisa Phillips

SEPTEMBER 30, 1659. I, POOR MISERABLE ROBINSON CRUSOE,

BEING SHIPWRECKED DURING A DREADFUL STORM,

IN THE OFFING, CAME ON SHORE

ON THIS DISMAL UNFORTUNATE ISLAND, WHICH I CALLED THE ISLAND OF DESPAIR,

ALL THE REST OF THE SHIP'S COMPANY BEING DROWNED,

AND MY SELF ALMOST DEAD.

—Daniel Defoe, Robinson Crusoe[1]

Robinson Crusoe is on a solitary sojourn, his shipwreck a punishment for defying his father, for seeking adventure instead of embracing the middle-class, status quo values his father had encouraged: "…the middle station of life was calculated for all kinds of virtues and all kinds of enjoyments… and is not exposed to the many vicissitudes as the higher or lower part of mankind."[2] Stranded on the deserted isle, Crusoe proceeds to subdue the wild environment, to tame it and establish his own kingdom of comfort and normalcy. He succeeds and is happy. Through ingenuity, adaptation, and improvisation he recreates his culture from nothing. As he plods his way through a long history of human technological invention, he solves almost every problem for himself. Crusoe is a testament to human resourcefulness and adaptability. Moreover, reduced to elementary needs in a simpler environment, Crusoe brings a new discernment to commonplace tasks: "'tis a little wonderful, and what I believe few people have thought much upon, viz., the strange multitude of little things necessary in the providing, producing, curing, dressing, making, and finishing this one article of bread."[3]

93

ROBINSON CRUSOE

1 Daniel Defoe, Robinson Crusoe
(London: Penguin Classics, 1985), (1719), 87.
2 Ibid., 28.
3 Ibid., 130.

DETAIL FROM
SELF-PORTRAIT WITH HOMEMADE CLOTHES, 1998

This is the kind of thing Charles Ray has thought about. Over the past two years, he has undertaken an exploration of the labor and craftsmanship required to produce the simple clothes and accessories that he puts on every day. Through an arduous process, he has disassembled his standard uniform to see how everything fits together. Then he has taught himself—through trial and error—to make patterns, sew clothes, fashion a good pair of rubber-soled shoes, as well as his own eyeglasses. Like Crusoe, he has remade the clothes he generally wears, by hand: from suede shoes, to jeans, plaid shirt, and jacket. One might wonder why an artist at the end of the twentieth century would choose to work like this, to return to the most rudimentary aspects of handicraft to make his own clothes? Ray's obsessive process is not dictated by survival needs like Crusoe's, but rather represents the self sufficiency and discipline that is at the heart of his artistic process.

Most important, like Crusoe (or Defoe), Ray forces us to reflect on things so basic or so close that we take them for granted. By subtly disrupting norms or changing the context of the ordinary, he causes a shift in perception and consciousness—an apprehension of the strangeness in the familiar that is the hallmark of his art. Told in great realism and detail, the ordinary becomes heroic; the simple becomes complex; the obvious becomes mysterious; the closed becomes open-ended; the literal becomes metaphorical. Appearances are shown to be deceptive: nothing is what it seems.

Ray's ultimate objective in making the clothes is to use them in a filmic self portrait, Self-Portrait with Homemade Clothes, still in progress. Ray says that the film will be simple, compressing two years of work into about ninety seconds of celluloid.[4] Without the reference in the title, the viewer won't know that the clothes are not store-bought. His "modeling" of the clothes will undoubtedly appear simple and "artless," hiding the complex process behind it. But before the filming has even begun, Ray's exploration has already yielded considerable rewards— a clearer understanding of the structure of things we take for granted; an appreciation of the skill involved in making a good product; and a keen sense of the sculptural and sensual qualities of each article of clothing and their intimate relation to his body.

95

4  "I'm a modern Robinson Crusoe, shipwrecked, abandoned, but self-sufficient in a contemporary media space." Charles Ray, interview with Lisa Phillips, 10 April, 1997, in Buflman, König, Matzner, ed., Sculpture. Projects in Münster, 1997 (Münster Westfälisches Landesmuseum, 1997), 332-335.

Louise Bourgeois, another artist who has used her clothing in her sculpture, maintains that: "Fashion is constructed, it is a context, a personal experience. It is not a concept. It is a repeated experience."[5] On the sculptural quality of clothes: "...[if] the garment is a sculpture of experience, then it is a sculpture that is realized in two stages: the first corresponds to the project of its construction and the second to its use, a species of sculpture that is created from the inside out, due to the experience of wearing it, of feeling its weight, of incorporating the contours and odors of the body, its memories and associations."[6] Ray has talked about the sexual experience of taking clothes apart, getting intimate with the "fit"—the relation of the forms to the parts of his body they fit around.[7]

At first Ray's body was an armature to hang the clothes on, but then the clothes became an armature to hang his portrait on. He has said that "the time and effort involved in making the clothes turned my body into an armature to show off my labor in the film, but then it flipped to the opposite and the clothes became an armature for my portrait. They gave me a formal grounding in the film and a reason to be there."[8] These kinds of reversals are common in Ray's work.

Clothes have been of recurring interest to Ray. *Self-Portrait with Homemade Clothes* harks back to one of Ray's earliest works, a photo piece documenting a performance titled *All My Clothes* (1973). Sixteen photographs showing Ray modeling every article of clothing he owns run side by side like a strip of celluloid film. In its deadpan, literal documentary presentation, it reads like a lexicon, a catalogue, an inventory, and recalls other photo conceptual works of that era by Bruce Nauman, Eleanor Antin, and Vito Acconci, who were also making performance works using their own bodies and photographing them. Ray also made another piece around the same time, showing a progression of his white clothes becoming dirtier and dirtier, gradually turning black. Ray siezed upon the repetition of the image in a sequence as a useful structure to hang his portrait, and psychology, on.

Over his twenty-five-year career, Ray has made many appearances in his work: as a living sculpture in performances; as an element connected to abstract objects (such as *In Memory of Sadat* [1981-85] where he is contained within a

IN MEMORY OF SADAT,
1981-85
COURTESY OF THE ARTIST

96

5 Louise Neri, "The Personal Effects of a Woman with No Secrets," in *Louise Bourgeois: Homesickness* (Yokohama: Yokohama Museum of Art, 1997), 141-145.

6 Ibid.

7 Charles Ray, in discussion with author, 10 April 1997.

8 Charles Ray, interview with Lisa Phillips, 10 April 1997, in *Sculpture. Projects in Münster 1997*, 334.

metal box with some of his limbs protruding); as a warped surface in the photo object Yes (1990); as a life-size, clothed mannequin; as a naked mannequin; making love to himself in a tableaux of replicas; contained inside a bottle; and as an actor in a celluloid projection. They are all self-portraits of a sort, but they are also oddly impersonal and emotionally detached. Although they bear his likeness, his self-portraits stand for everyman—singular, yet utterly common-place, devoid of personal expression.

In Puzzle Bottle (1995), completed just before the clothes odyssey, a wooden effigy of the artist stands mutely staring outwards. The artist is contained and isolated inside a bottle—a metaphorical castaway or message in a bottle. This amusing and unlikely self-portrait uses the ship-in-the-bottle method of rigging up several small parts to complete the whole. Though very tiny in scale, it has a big and hypnotic presence, in part due to the internal space. The idea came to Ray when he was trying to make an abstract sculpture and kept running into problems. He was about to give up when he saw a photo of Anthony Caro's Early One Morning (1962) on his bookcase: "On this particular day there was a cider bottle turned sideways in front of the photograph. Looking at it through the cider jug gave me the idea of building a sculpture in a bottle. Eventually I built my portrait in a bottle and the space became abstract while the sculpture itself turned figurative."[9] As in Self-Portrait with Homemade Clothes, the artist is marooned, stranded, "outside of time," "corked up." (It is no accident that these allusions to shipwreck, castaway, seafaring apply, since Ray's major leisure activity is sailing and he spends long periods of time on his sailboat.)

From the start, Ray's work has always demonstrated autonomous completeness—a self-sufficiency and self-containment that has been much commented on. The self-portrait is one genre that keeps cropping up in Ray's art as a metaphor for this autonomy. Yet autonomy is also the central modernist paradigm, and Ray has had a long-standing interest in modernist sculpture such as Caro's—and particular admiration for Minimalism, arguably the last moment of modernism. He shares the Minimalists' love of the gestalt, and their repetition of unitary forms—the pared down, essential, and generic object. He also

ANTHONY CARO
EARLY ONE MORNING,
1962
TATE GALLERY, LONDON

9 Ibid., 333.

RAY ON HIS SAILBOAT

shares their denial of emotional expressiveness. This may partly derive from his experience in military school where he was expected to hide his life behind conformity—to keep his room and locker just like everyone else, according to code.

Three cubic works, Ink Box (1986), 7½-Ton Cube (1990), and 32x33x35=34x33x35 (1989), look like Minimalist sculptures from a distance. But these works tweak the "dumb" quality, or geometric purity of the generic cube through some unexpected element or perceptual trick. The Ink Box is filled with printers' ink—though its surface looks like the smooth completion of the cubic form. The 7½-Ton Cube carries as much weight as it is possible to compress into that form. It is a solid steel cube painted white to appear much lighter than it really is. 32x33x35=34x33x35, apparently a perfectly square box from the outside, is actually sunk into the floor, its bottom hidden from view until you look inside. These works are phenomenological and perceptual encounters that engage the viewer in space and time. While Ray has affection and nostalgia for a time when sculpture was sculpture, and admiration for the authority, for the rigor and idealism and belief in purity that the Minimalists upheld (and conviction in art's radical power), he is also skeptical about their utopian ideals in a dystopic era, and presents them as illusions. Their icons of authority were also used by Ray as foils for psychological states he wanted to express.

Ink Line (1987) could be a simple line or thread drawn from floor to ceiling—but it is ink in perpetual motion, circulating in a thin stream between the two horizontal planes. Rotating Circle (1988) also appears to be a white on white circle drawn on the wall. In fact, it is a disc spinning so fast that its movement cannot be detected by the naked eye. Both of these works contain the potential of disruption and provoke anxiety as soon as you realize what they are: material in action. Again, things do not appear as they seem.

Sculpture is not static and idealized for Ray, but a temporal medium. All of his work comes out of what he calls "the wildness of the event."[10] Even when he works with imagery, it's about the relationship of people to things, bodies to objects. Figure and experience are key. Ray has said that for him, "sculpture is a verb."[11] His work has strong affinities with process art—like that of Richard Serra,

10 Joan Hugo, "Between Object and Persona," High Performance 30 (1985): 27, 29.
11 Charles Ray, in discussion with the author.

who in 1967–68 compiled a list of verbs ("to roll, to crease, to fold...") that he went on to use as the basis of actual sculpture. Ray's attitude about the "event" also comes out of Performance Art and his own early performances in the 1970s. As a student, he excelled at mountain climbing and sailing, both solitary physical activities. In the studio, he felt more comfortable moving around and moving things around. He felt a connection to action painting in his performances and came to view making sculpture as behavioral. His idea of sculpture also corresponds to the "condition of theater" that Michael Fried derisively ascribed to the Minimalists in the 1960s: the action and movement required of the viewer to experience the work—the durational relation between subject and object.[12]

As much as Ray admires Minimalist sculptors like Donald Judd and Robert Morris, he also deflates them and satirizes them through his interventions and peculiar self-projections. Again, he is drawn to their readymade structures of authority in order to bring another, psychological dimension to them. Some critics have charged that the Minimalists' rhetoric of radicality—their use of "strong" and "aggressive" materials, in fact disguised an exaltation of male expressions of power—the strong, the forceful, the authoritative, the commanding.[13] In a work like Self-Portrait, Ray cleverly reverses these values, offering up the opposite image—an alternative "man": ordinary, anti-heroic, unaggressive, a vulnerable and awkward man. Ray's image and wardrobe suggests a middle-class, Midwestern "guy" with a casual, sporty, outdoorsman quality, yet decidedly plain and generic.

In this commonplace effect, there is also an allusion to the mass produced, post-human on the techno-horizon, which provides another ironic twist on Minimalism's ethic of mass production. In Oh! Charley, Charley, Charley... (1992), Ray replaces standardized industrial materials with industrially produced man— the cyborg— and all the post-human ontologies such a creature implies. Here, with his typical perverse and deadpan wit, he has used his own form as the unit repeated in a baroquely composed "daisy chain." Eight Ray replicants are involved in a sex orgy—the penultimate commentary on autonomy and tautology. As he uses his own form as ordinary, generic material, Ray himself is the

DONALD JUDD, UNTITLED, 1968
WHITNEY MUSEUM OF AMERICAN ART, NEW YORK
PURCHASE WITH FUNDS FROM
THE HOWARD AND JEAN LIPMAN FOUNDATION, INC.

ROBERT MORRIS, UNTITLED (L-BEAMS), 1965
WHITNEY MUSEUM OF AMERICAN ART, NEW YORK
PURCHASE WITH FUNDS FROM
THE HOWARD AND JEAN LIPMAN FOUNDATION, INC.

99

12 Michael Fried, "Art and Objecthood," Artforum (Summer 1967): 12-23.
13 Anna Chave, "Minimalism and the Rhetoric of Power," Arts Magazine 64 (January 1990): 44-63.

UNPAINTED SCULPTURE, 1997
WALKER ART CENTER, MINNEAPOLIS

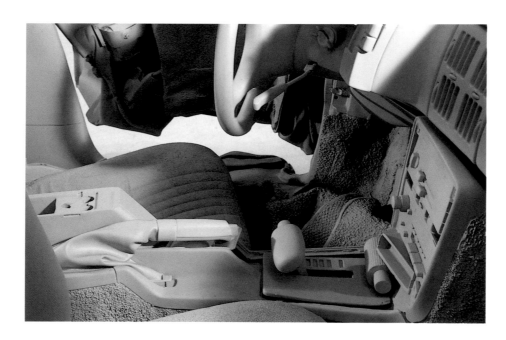

DETAIL, UNPAINTED SCULPTURE, 1997

interchangeable vessel—the neutered, neutral standard consumer good. He is there but absent, presenting himself as a still life—a dead, wooden, and artificial creation of the cultural. What these works question is the uniqueness of identity in an age of mass produced "identities." They present an indeterminate and anxious subject whose body is a convention of cultural construction.

Many of Ray's later works make use of inflected images from mass culture —cars, fire trucks, mannequins—prompting the inevitable associations with Pop Art. What Pop Art shares with Minimalism, of course, is an interest in the readymade. Ray extends this tradition: his subject matter is highly inflected like Pop Art, but his presentation is obdurate and standardized in the Minimalist mode. Much like Warhol, to whom he has recently been compared, there is tension between the public form and highly personal content. It is this contradiction that gives his work such great tension and expressive power. [14]

In a recent work, Unpainted Sculpture (1997), Ray began with an automobile wreck salvaged from a fatal crash. Then, in a process similar to the fabrication of his homemade clothes, he began the painstaking, two-year task of disassembling the Pontiac Grand Am, part by part, casting each piece (over one hundred of them) in fiberglass. In the process of getting intimate with every square inch of the auto body, Ray could appreciate the forms made by pure chance and brought out passages of abstraction with a gray monochromatic topcoat. There are several contradictions at work here, among them the creating of an object that has been totally destroyed. "It's starting its life over again as an art object.... It has a funny trail of identity from the factory in Detroit through wrecks, then ending up in my hands, on another weird assembly line in the studio and going back out again."[15] Another contradiction is that a dead object—an unusable automobile in which someone has been killed—has a lively, active, and expressionistic surface. The frontal impact has sent the hood billowing backwards into the front seat and popped the rear doors askew. Furthermore, Unpainted Sculpture is indeed painted a flat gray to give it the unified and abstract quality of a model. This is a work about action, life, death and resurrection.

The curious thing about Unpainted Sculpture is Ray's attention to the

14 Bruce Hainley, "Charles Ray: Regen Projects," Artforum (January 1998): 91.
15 Dennis Cooper, interview with Charles Ray, Index (January 1998): 41.

abstract elements and his distance from the violent event that produced the form. When questioned about the unavoidable resonance with both Princess Diana's death and the recently released David Cronenberg movie Crash, based on the J.G. Ballard novel, Ray responds: "The topicality of the car wreck is a counterpoint to the abstraction."[16] Ray has acknowledged the influence of Ballard on his thinking—particularly on his figurative work and in the sketching out of a new relationship between sex and technology. Technology serves to remove and abstract the body, perversely idealizing it and objectifying it through distance. Ray remembers finding mannequin catalogues more pornographic than Playboy or Hustler.

Crash is a novel about the merging of bodies and machines and a subculture's lustful devotion to crashes both spontaneous and engineered. Ballard observed that Vaughan, the novel's protagonist:

> UNFOLDED FOR ME ALL HIS OBSESSIONS WITH THE MYSTERIOUS EROTICISM OF
> WOUNDS: THE PERVERSE LOGIC OF BLOOD-SOAKED INSTRUMENT PANELS, SEAT-
> BELTS SMEARED WITH EXCREMENT, SUN VISORS LINED WITH BRAIN TISSUE. FOR
> VAUGHAN EACH CRASHED CAR SET OFF A TREMOR OF EXCITEMENT, IN THE COMPLEX
> GEOMETRIES OF A DENTED FENDER, IN THE UNEXPECTED VARIATIONS OF CRUSHED
> RADIATOR GRILLES, IN THE GROTESQUE OVERHANG OF AN INSTRUMENT PANEL
> FORCED ON TO A DRIVER'S CROTCH AS IF IN SOME CALIBRATED ACT OF MACHINE
> FELLATIO. THE INTIMATE TIME AND SPACE OF A SINGLE HUMAN BEING HAD BEEN
> FOSSILIZED FOREVER IN THIS WEB OF CHROMIUM KNIVES AND FROSTED GLASS.[17]

Unpainted Sculpture, like so many of Ray's works, seems to cry out for a psychological reading. Though he recognizes the appeal of shock value and surprise ("the uncanniness draws people in"[18]) he usually focuses his discussion on spatial issues. In spite of the fact that formal aspects of space have dominated his own descriptions of the work, (he would appear to be most interested in "the complex geometries of a dented fender"), all of Ray's work is about bodies. Even when the body is not literally present it is implied by the object or situation or perceptual conundrum. Throughout Ray's work there is a sense of the body as a sculptural object and the sculptural object as a body—a sense of self as

ROBERT GOBER, LEG WITH CANDLE, 1991
WHITNEY MUSEUM OF AMERICAN ART, NEW YORK
PURCHASE WITH FUNDS FROM
ROBERT W. WILSON

16 Ibid., 41
17 Andrea Vale, ed. Re/Search, J.G. Ballard issue (San Francisco: Research Publishing, 1984): 73.
18 Dennis Cooper, 42.
19 Klaus Kertess, "Some Bodies," Parkett, no. 38 (September 1993): 37.

sculpture and sculpture as self.[19]

During the past two decades, the strongest, most consistently compelling and provocative sculpture has been figurative—from Bruce Nauman and Louise Bourgeois to Robert Gober, Jeff Koons, Matthew Barney, and Kiki Smith—and of course, Charles Ray. Ray and his peers are obsessive objectmakers whose work is hallucinogenic, psychologically eerie and reflects the luxury of "dreaming time." They are sculptors influenced by performance and environment and the growing schism between nature and culture. They are artists for whom traditional categories and binary thinking do not apply.

Another observation from Ballard provides insight into the orientation of Ray and some of his contemporaries:

> IN THE PAST WE HAVE ALWAYS ASSUMED THAT THE EXTERNAL WORLD AROUND US
> HAS REPRESENTED REALITY, HOWEVER CONFUSING OR UNCERTAIN, AND THAT
> THE INNER WORLD OF OUR MINDS, ITS DREAMS, HOPES, AMBITIONS, REPRESENTED
> THE REALM OF FANTASY AND THE IMAGINATION  THESE ROLES, TOO, IT SEEMS TO ME,
> HAVE BEEN REVERSED. THE MOST PRUDENT AND EFFECTIVE METHOD OF DEALING
> WITH THE WORLD AROUND US IS TO ASSUME THAT IT IS A COMPLETE FICTION—
> CONVERSELY, THE ONE SMALL NODE OF REALITY LEFT TO US IS INSIDE OUR OWN
> HEADS. FREUD'S CLASSIC DISTINCTION BETWEEN THE LATENT AND MANIFEST
> CONTENT OF THE DREAM, BETWEEN THE APPARENT AND THE REAL, NOW NEEDS
> TO BE APPLIED TO THE EXTERNAL WORLD OF SO-CALLED REALITY.[20]

For an artist like Ray, who lives in his head, traditional distinctions do not hold: in his object lessons, common dualities like traditional/vanguard, abstract/real, mind/body, animate/inanimate, private/social, are collapsed or inverted. This may partly explain why for a long time, Ray's work eluded public and critical attention. At first, few people knew what to make of his peculiar hybrid of Minimalism and Pop, Surrealism, Photorealism, Conceptualism, and Performance Art. But his anomalous array of media and genres is now recognized as characteristic of the stylistic hybridity that typifies so much late twentieth-century art. Like Crusoe remaking his life, Ray has taken on traditional genres and recast them to show us their truly strange nature and weird beauty. By literalizing the real, Ray

20 Re/Search, J.G. Ballard issue, 98.

crosses back into illusion and metaphor. He has described his work repeatedly in this way: "[I was] trying to make something that was so abstract it became real or so real that it became abstract. [When] you go in so far, you come out the other side."[21] Ray's work is like a footprint in the sand, in its ability to surprise, inspire contemplation and keep us humble.

> IT HAPPENED ONE DAY ABOUT NOON GOING TOWARDS MY BOAT, I WAS EXCEEDINGLY SURPRISED WITH THE PRINT OF A MAN'S NAKED FOOT ON THE SHORE, WHICH WAS VERY PLAIN TO BE SEEN IN THE SAND. I STOOD LIKE ONE THUNDERSTRUCK, OR AS IF I HAD SEEN AN APPARITION: I LISTENED, I LOOKED 'ROUND ME, I COULD HEAR NOTHING NOR SEE ANYTHING; I WENT UP TO A RISING GROUND TO LOOK FARTHER; I WENT UP THE SHORE AND DOWN THE SHORE, BUT IT WAS ALL ONE, I COULD SEE NO OTHER IMPRESSION BUT THAT ONE.[22]

THOMAS STOTHART,
ROBINSON CRUSOE AND THE FOOTPRINT, 1790

21 Lucinda Barnes, "Interview with Charles Ray", in *Charles Ray* (Newport Harbor Art Museum, 1990), 12.
22 Daniel Defoe, *Robinson Crusoe*, 162.

# EXHIBITION CHRONOLOGY

## ONE-PERSON EXHIBITIONS

### 1998

"Charles Ray," Whitney Museum of American Art, June 4-October 11; The Museum of Contemporary Art, Los Angeles, November 15, 1998-February 21, 1999; Museum of Contemporary Art, Chicago, June 21-September, 1999.

### 1997

Regen Projects, Los Angeles, October 18-November 29.

### 1996

Studio Guenzani, Milan.

### 1994

"Charles Ray," Rooseum-Center for Contemporary Art, Malmö, March 5-May 8; ICA, London, June 24-August 14; Kunsthalle Bern & Kunsthalle Zürich, August 28-October 9.

### 1993

Feature, New York.  Galerie Metropole, Vienna.

### 1992

Donald Young Gallery, Seattle.  Feature, New York.

### 1991

Galerie Claire Burrus, Paris.  Feature, New York. Galerie Metropole, Vienna.

### 1990

Burnett Miller Gallery, Los Angeles.  Interim Art, London. Feature, New York.  "Charles Ray," Newport Harbor Art Museum, Newport Beach.  Matrix Gallery, University Art Museum, University of California at Berkeley, Berkeley.

### 1989

Burnett Miller Gallery, Los Angeles.  Feature, New York. The Mattress Factory, Pittsburgh.

### 1988

Feature, Chicago.  Burnett Miller Gallery, Los Angeles.

### 1987

Feature, Chicago.  Burnett Miller Gallery, Los Angeles.

### 1985

Mercer Union, Toronto, Ontario.  New Langton Arts, San Francisco.

### 1983

64 Market Street, Venice.

## SELECTED GROUP EXHIBITIONS

### 1997

"A Lasting Legacy: Selections from the Lannan Foundation Gift," The Museum of Contemporary Art, Los Angeles, September 7, 1997-January 4, 1998.  "Biennale de Lyon d'art contemporain," Maison de Lyon, France, July 7-September 24.  "Skulptur. Projekte in Münster 1997," Westfälisches Landesmuseum für Kunst und Kulturgeschichte, Münster, June 22- September 28.  "Objects of Desire: The Modern Still Life," The Museum of Modern Art, New York, May 21-August 26. "Sunshine & Noir: Art in L.A. 1960-1997," Louisiana Museum of Modern Art, Humlebaek, May 16-September 7; Kunstmuseum Wolfsburg, Wolfsburg, November 15-February 1, 1998; Castello di Rivoli, Rivoli, May 8-August 23, 1998; and The Armand Hammer Museum, Los Angeles, September 16, 1998-January 1999.  "1997 Whitney Biennial Exhibition," Whitney Museum of American Art, New York, March 20-June 15.  "Veronica's Revenge: Selections from the Lambert Art Collection", Centre d'Art Contemporain, Geneva, February 28-May 11.

### 1996

"Just Past: The Contemporary in the Permanent Collection, 1975-96," The Museum of Contemporary Art, Los Angeles, September 28-January 7.  "Portrait of the Artist," Anthony d'Offay Gallery, London. "Distemper: Dissonant Themes in the Art of the 1990s," Hirshhorn Museum and Sculptural Garden, Smithsonian Institution, Washington, D.C., June 20-September 15.  "Art at the End of the 20th Century: Selections from the Whitney Museum of American Art," National Gallery, Athens, June 10-September 30; Museu d'Art Contemporani, Barcelona, December 18-April 6, 1997; Kunstmuseum Bonn, June-September 1997.  "NowHere: Walking and Thinking and Walking," Louisiana Museum of Modern Art, Humlebaek, May 15-September 8.  "Happy End," Kunsthalle Düsseldorf, Düsseldorf.  "Young Americans: Part II," Saatchi Gallery, London.  "Narcissism: Artists Reflect Themselves," California Center for the Arts Museum, Escondido.

## 1995

"1995 Whitney Biennial," Whitney Museum of American Art, New York. "Private/Public: ARS 1995," Museum of Contemporary Art, Helsinki, February 11-May 28. "MicroMegas: Miniatures and Monstrosities in Contemporary Art," The Israel Museum, Jersualem. "PerForms: Janine Antoni, Charles Ray, Jana Sterbak," Institute of Contemporary Art, Philadelphia, September 9-November 5. "Féminin-masculin: le sexe de l'art," Centre Georges Pompidou, Paris. "Everything That's Interesting is New," The Dakis Joannou Collection, Athens School of Fine Art, Athens. "Still Leben," National Museum, Stockholm, February 1-May 1. "A Glimpse of the Norton Collection as Revealed by Kim Dingle," Santa Monica Museum of Art, December 10, 1995-February 26, 1996; Site Santa Fe, September 13-November 2

## 1994

"Radical Scavenger(s): The Conceptual Vernacular in Recent American Art," Museum of Contemporary Art, Chicago, February 7-April 17. "Face-Off: The Portrait in Recent Art," Institute of Contemporary Art, University of Pennsylvania, Philadelphia, September 9-October 30; Joslyn Art Museum, Omaha, January 28-March 19, 1995; Weatherspoon Art Gallery, University of North Carolina, Greensboro, April 9-May 28, 1995.

## 1993

"1993 Whitney Biennial," Whitney Museum of American Art, New York. "Biennale of Sydney," Art Gallery of New South Wales and Bond Store 3/4, Sydney. "Tables, Selections from the Lannan Foundation Collections," Lannan Art Foundation, Los Angeles. "Images, Selections from the Lannan Foundation Collections," Lannan Art Foundation, Los Angeles. "Seeing the Forest Through the Trees," Contemporary Arts Museum, Houston.

## 1992

"Dirty Data Sammlung Schurmann," Ludwig Forum für internationale Kunst, Cologne. "Spiral Gallery," Wacoal Art Center, Tokyo. "Strange Developments," Anthony d'Offay Gallery, London. "Images," Lannan Art Foundation, Los Angeles. "The Other Side," Tony Shafrazi Gallery, New York. "Viaggio a Los Angeles," Castello di Rivara, Rivara. "Post Human," FAE Musée d'Art Contemporain, Pully/Lausanne; Castello di Rivoli, Museo d'Arte Contemporanea, Rivoli; DESTE Foundation for Contemporary Art, Athens; Deichtorhallen Hamburg, Hamburg. "Documenta IX," Kassel. "Helter Skelter: L.A. Art in the 1990s," The Museum of Contemporary Art, Los Angeles, January 26-April 26. Donald Young Gallery, Seattle. The Sydney Biennial, Sydney.

## 1991

"The Savage Garden," Sala de Exposiciones de la Fundation Caja de Pensiores, Madrid. "Cadences: Icon and Abstraction in Context," The New Museum of Contemporary Art, New York. "Mechanika," The Contemporary Arts Center, Cincinnati. Galerie Max Hetzler, Cologne. "Devices," Josh Baer Gallery, New York. "Katharina Fritsch, Robert Gober, Reinhard Mucha, Charles Ray, and Rachel Whiteread," Luhring Augustine Gallery, New York.

## 1990

"Fifth Anniversary Exhibition," Burnett Miller Gallery, Los Angeles. "Recent Drawings," Whitney Museum of American Art, New York. Matrix Gallery, University Art Museum, University of California at Berkeley, Berkeley. "Blood Remembering," Snug Harbor Cultural Center, Staten Island. "Heart in Mouth," Fahey/Klein Gallery, Los Angeles. Donald Young Gallery, Chicago.

## 1989

"1989 Biennial Exhibition," Whitney Museum of American Art, New York. "Loaded," Kuhlenschmidt Gallery, Los Angeles.

## 1988

"Near Miss," Feature, Chicago. "Still Trauma," Milford Gallery, New York. 303 Gallery, New York. "Selections From the Permanent Collection," Newport Harbor Art Museum, Newport Beach. "Recent Art From Los Angeles," Cleveland Center for Contemporary Art, Cleveland.

## 1987

"Industrial Icons," University Art Gallery, San Diego State University, San Diego. "Nature," Feature, Chicago. Burnett Miller Gallery, Los Angeles.

## 1986

"Baaa Baaa Ba'bel," Alexandria Hotel, Los Angeles. Frederick A. Wight Gallery, University of California at Los Angeles, Los Angeles.

## 1984

Los Angeles Institute of Contemporary Art, Los Angeles.

## 1981

Cape Gallery, New Orleans.

## 1980

Uno Gallery, New Orleans. Contemporary Arts Center, New Orleans.

# BIBLIOGRAPHY

## BOOKS AND CATALOGUES

Art at the End of the 20th Century: Selections from the Whitney Museum of American Art. Exh. cat. New York: Whitney Museum of American Art, 1996. Essay by Johanna Drucker.

Barnes, Lucinda, ed. Charles Ray. Exh. cat. Newport Beach, California: Newport Harbor Art Museum, 1990.

Benezra, Neal, and Olga M. Viso. Distemper: Dissonant Themes in the Art of the 1990s. Exh. cat. Washington, D.C.: Hirshhorn Museum and Sculpture Garden, Smithsonian Institution, 1996.

Bussmann, Klaus, Kasper König, and Florian Matzner, eds. Sculpture. Projects in Münster 1997. Exh. cat. Münster, Germany: Verlag Gerd Hatje, 1998.

Cameron, Dan. El jardin savaje (The Savage Garden). Exh. cat. Madrid: Fundación Caja de Pensiones, 1991.

Cavelli-Bjorkman, Görel. Still Leben (Still Lifes). Exh. cat. Stockholm: Nationalmuseum, 1995.

Corrias, Pilar. The Banal That Turns Disquieting: A Discussion on the Work of Charles Ray. Masters' Thesis, 1994.

Deitch, Jeffrey. Everything That's Interesting Is New: The Dakis Joannou Collection. Athens: DESTE Foundation for Contemporary Art, and Stuttgart: Cantz Verlag, 1996.

—————. Young Americans: New American Art in the Saatchi Collection. Exh. cat. London: Saatchi Gallery, 1996.

Farm. Exh. cat. Chicago: Feature, and Instituting Contemporary Idea, 1987.

Feldman, Melissa E. Face-Off: The Portrait in Recent Art. Exh. cat. Philadelphia: Institute of Contemporary Art, University of Pennsylvania, 1994. Essay by Benjamin H. D. Buchloh.

Féminin-masculin: le sexe de l'art (Feminine-Masculine: The Sex of Art). Exh. cat. Paris: Centre Georges Pompidou, and Gallimard/Electa, 1995.

Ferguson, Bruce W. Charles Ray. Exh. cat. Mälmo, Sweden: Rooseum-Center for Contemporary Art, 1994.

Ferguson, Bruce W. NowHere. Exh. cat. Humlebaek, Denmark: Louisiana Museum of Modern Art, 1996.

Freeman, Phyllis et al. New Art. New York: Abrams Inc., 1990.

Guidi, Anna Cestelli. La "documenta" di Kassel. Milan: Costa & Nolan, 1997.

Kertess, Klaus et al. 1995 Biennial Exhibition. Exh. cat. New York: Whitney Museum of American Art, and Abrams Inc., 1995.

Kunsthalle Bern, 1994: Jahresbericht des Vereins Kunsthalle Bern. Bern: Kunsthalle, 1994.

Mechanika. Exh. cat. Cincinnati: The Contemporary Arts Center, 1991.

Narcissism: Artists Reflect Themselves. Exh. cat. Escondido: California Center for the Arts Museum, 1996.

Nature. Chicago: Feature, 1987.

1989 Biennial Exhibition. Exh. cat. New York: Whitney Museum of American Art, 1989. Texts by Richard Armstrong, John G. Hanhardt, Richard Marshall, and Lisa Phillips.

Nittve, Lars, and Helle Crenzien. Sunshine & Noir: Art in L.A. 1960-1997. Exh. cat. Humlebaek, Denmark: Louisiana Museum of Modern Art, 1997. Texts by Anne Ayres, Laura Cottingham, Mike Davis, Russell Ferguson, William R. Hackman, Timothy Martin, Terry R. Myers, Nittve, and Peter Schjeldahl.

Perchuk, Andrew, and Helaine Posner, eds. The Masculine Masquerade: Masculinity and Representation. Cambridge, Massachusetts: MIT List Visual Arts Center, and The MIT Press, 1995.

Phillips, Lisa, and Louise Neri. 1997 Biennial Exhibition. Exh. cat. New York: Whitney Museum of American Art, and Abrams Inc., 1997.

Recent Drawings. Exh. cat. New York: Whitney Museum of American Art, 1990.

Rowell, Margit. Objects of Desire: The Modern Still Life. Exh. cat. New York: The Museum of Modern Art, 1997.

Sangster, Gary. Cadences: Icons and Abstraction in Context. Exh. cat. New York: The New Museum of Contemporary Art, 1991.

Schimmel, Paul. Helter Skelter: L.A. Art in the 1990s. Exh. cat. Los Angeles: The Museum of Contemporary Art, 1992. Essays by Norman M. Klein and Lane Relyea.

Schwabsky, Barry, ed. Radical Scavenger(s): The Conceptual Vernacular in Recent American Art. Exh. cat. Chicago: Museum of Contemporary Art, 1994.

Sobel, Dean. Identity Crisis: Self-Portraiture at the End of the Century. Exh. cat. Milwaukee: Milwaukee Art Museum, 1998.

Sussman Elizabeth et al. 1993 Biennial Exhibition. Exh. cat. New York: Whitney Museum of American Art, and Abrams Inc., 1993.

Tannenbaum, Judith. PerForms: Janine Antoni, Charles Ray, Jana Sterbak. Exh. cat. Philadelphia: Institute of Contemporary Art, University of Pennsylvania, 1995. Essay by Brian Wallis.

Tucker, Marcia. Choices: Making an Art of Everyday Life. Exh. cat. New York: The New Museum of Contemporary Art, 1986.

Yksityinen/Julkinen (Private/Public): Ars 95. Exh. cat. Helsinki: National Museum, 1995.

## PERIODICALS

Adams, Brooks. "Shock of the Mundane." Vogue 180, no. 3 (March 1990): 344-350.

Aliaga, Juan V cente. "Le jardin sauvage." Art Press (France), no. 157 (April 1991): 86.

"All Photo Issue." High Performance 5, no. 4 (1983): 48.

"Art. The New Yorker (April 27, 1992): 13.

"Art around Town." 7 Days 2, no. 19 (May 17, 1989): 69.

"Arte." El Pais (January 20, 1991): 35.

"Artist Gallery." LA Style (July 1986): 38.

Auerbach, Lisa Anne. "Charles Ray at Regen Projects." L.A. Weekly (1997): 51.

Ayres, Anne. "Kassel Fax." Art Issues, no. 24 (September-October 1992): 34-35.

Birnbaum, Daniel. "Walking and Thinking and Walking Incandescent." frieze (Great Britain) no. 30 (September-October 1996): 52-53.

—————. "Ultra Swede: Conversation with Lars Nittve." Artforum 34, no. 5 (January 1996): 23-24, 99.

Blas, Parrington. "Question About Abstraction." Figaro (October 27, 1980): 28.

Bonami, Francesco. "Charles Ray." Flash Art (Italian Edition) 24, no. 169 (1992): 56-59 and front cover.

—————. "Charles Ray: A Telephone Conversation." Flash Art 25, no. 165 (Summer 1992): 98-100.

—————. "Panorama NYC." Flash Art 25, no. 166 (October 1992): 130-131.

Brown, Gerard. "Discussion After The Show: The ICA's exhibit of objects created by performance artists begs for interpretation." Philadelphia Weekly (October 25, 1995): 38.

Brougher, Nora Halpern. "Charles Ray." Flash Art 23, no. 155 (November-December 1990): 152.

"Calendar Section." NOW (March 14, 1985): 28.

Callahan, Joe. "Controversial Art Exhibit Shocks." The Bi-College News (September 30, 1995): 12.

Cameron, Dan. "Backlash." Artforum 31, no. 9 (May 1993): 12-13.

Cavina, Desideria. "Personaggi delle favole vittoriane per l'Aids." Arte (April 18, 1993): 25.

"Charles Ray." Geijutsu Shincho (Japan) (June 1993): 42-47.

"Charles Ray." Newport Harbor Art Museum Calendar (July-August 1990).

"Charles Ray in Rooseum Spotlight." Flash Art News (May 1994): 49.

Clothier, Peter. "Charles Ray: Edgy Provocative Presences." Art News 86, no. 10 (December 1987): 97-98.

————. "Charles Ray: In the Black." Artspace 14, no. 6 (September-October 1990): 63.

Conti, Marina. "Gridatelo con la Horror Art." L'Espresso (March 7, 1993): 114-117.

Conti, Rena, and Ivan Moskowitz. "The Salad Years?" L.A. Muscle (February-March 1997): 19.

Cooper, Dennis. "Charles Ray with Dennis Cooper." Index (Sweden) (January-February 1998): 38-46.

Cortijo, Paco. "El jardin savaje de la caixa." Mecenazjo (February 23, 1991): 36-37.

Csaszar, Tom. "PerForms: Janine Antoni, Charles Ray, Jana Sterbak." Sculpture (March 1996): 57.

Damsgard, Helle. "Charles Ray." Index, no. 2 (June 1994).

Dickerson, Paul. "Charles Ray." Bomb, no. 52 (Summer 1995): 42-47. Interview.

Drohojowska, Hunter. "Charles Ray's Way." L.A. Weekly (April 15, 1983): 12.

————. "Pick of the Week." L.A. Weekly (October 19, 1984).

————. "L.A. Raw." Art News 91, no. 4 (April 1992): 78-81.

"Il Post-Uomo senza quality." Vernissage (November 1992): 1-3 and front cover.

Erickson, Peter. "Seeing White." Transition: An International Review, no. 67 (Fall 1995): 166-185.

Ewert, Mark, and Mitchell Watkins, eds. Ruh Roh!, no. 1 (Winter 1992): 40-41.

"Faces to Watch in '98: Here's Who'll Be Who." Los Angeles Times (December 28, 1997): 5.

Ferguson, Bruce. "Everything That's Interesting Is New." Flash Art 29, no. 187 (March-April 1996): 108-109.

Flynn, Leo. "Law and the Erotic." Art & Design: Abstract Eroticism: Touch Me (London) (1996): 70-81.

Frank, Peter. "Art Pick of the Week." L.A. Weekly (August 31, 1990).

————. "USA: Blickpunkt Westcoast." Kunstforum International (Belgium), no. 119 (1992): 175-178 and 292-295.

Fricke, Harald. "NowHere: Louisiana Museum." Artforum 35, no. 3 (November 1996): 95, 127.

Galloway, David. "Documenta: Missing Edge." International Herald Tribune (June 27-28, 1992): 6.

Gandee, Charles. "People are talking about state of the art." Vogue 183, no. 3 (March 1993): 101.

Gardner, Colin. "The Art Galleries." Los Angeles Times (March 6, 1987): 18.

————. "Four Examples of Illusion: Richard Baker, Charles Ray, Lauri Sing, Fred Tomaselli." Artweek 15, no. 36 (October 27, 1984): 1.

Geer, Suvan. "Marked By Art: Charles Ray at Newport Harbor Art Museum." Artweek 21, no. 28 (September 6, 1990): 1, 20.

Glanzer, Elizabeth. "Charles Ray: Evolving Anxiety from the Shadows." Orange Coast Daily Pilot (August 5, 1990): C5.

"Goings on About Town." The New Yorker (May 22, 1989).

"Goings on About Town." The New Yorker (June 4, 1990): 18.

"Goings on About Town." The New Yorker (May 18, 1992): 16.

"Goings on About Town." The New Yorker (June 29, 1992): 10.

Goldberger, Paul. "Klaus Kertess: The Art of His Choosing." The New York Times Magazine (February 26, 1995): 30-39, 52, 55, 61, 62.

Hackett, Regina. "Charles Ray Still Snubs Convention." Seattle Post-Intelligencer (June 3, 1992): C3.

Hainley, Bruce. "Charles Ray: Regen Projects." Artforum 56, no. 5 (January 1998): 91.

Harvey, Doug. "Charles Ray at Regen Projects." Art Issues, no. 51 (January-February 1998): 36.

Hasli, Richard. "Der Puppenspieler." Neue Zürcher Zeitung (September 9, 1994): 45.

Heartney, Eleanor. "Dossier: FIAC 93, New York, dans les galeries." Art Press (France), no. 184 (October 1994): 24-28.

————. "Identity Politics at the Whitney." Art in America 81, no. 5 (May 1993) 43-47.

"Helter Skelter: L.A. Art in the 1990's." The Contemporary (The Museum of Contemporary Art, Los Angeles) (December-January 1992): 7 and front cover.

Hess, Elizabeth. "Up Against the Wall." The Village Voice (March 16, 1993): 35, 38.

Hirsch, Jeffrey. "Works in Progress: A Portfolio." L.A. Style (June 1990): 186.

Hoving, Thomas. "Art for the Ages." Cigar Aficionado (Summer 1995): 214-226.

Hughes, Robert. "A Fiesta of Whining." Time (March 1993): 68-69.

Hugo, Joan. "Between Object and Persona: The Sculpture Events of Charles Ray." High Performance 8, no. 2 (1985): 26-29.

"In Defense of Literature." Frank, no. 4 (Summer-Autumn 1987): 63.

Intra, Giovanni. "Charles Ray: Regen Projects." Flash Art (January-February 1998): 117.

Jaunin, Françoise. "Posthuman." Voir (June 1992): 26-27.

Jermanok, Stephen. "In Profile: Robert Storr." Art & Antiques 19, no. 7 (Summer 1996): 144.

Jimenez, Pablo. "Un jardin entre la vida y el arte." ABC (January 24, 1991): 123.

Kandel, Susan. "L.A. in Review." Arts Magazine 66, no. 8 (April 1992): 98-99.

Kazanjian, Dodie. "Ray Beyond Cool." Vogue 185, no. 9 (September 1995): 556-600.

Kelly, Mike. "Foul Perfection: Thoughts on Caricature." Artforum 27, no. 5 (January 1989): 92-99.

Kent, Sarah. "Charles Ray." Time Out (14-21 November 1990): 32.

Kertess, Klaus. "Recent Drawing." Whitney Museum of Art Calendar (February-May 1990).

————. "Some Bodies." Parkett (Switzerland), no. 37 (September 1993): 36-45.

Kimmelman, Michael. "At Documenta, It's Survival of the Loudest." The New York Times 141, no. 2 (July 5, 1992): H27.

————. "Helter Skelter Reveals the Evil of Banality." The New York Times (March 22, 1992): H37.

————. "Is Duane Hanson the Phidias of Our Time?" The New York Times 143, no. 2 (February 27, 1994): H39.

————. "A Whitney Biennial That's Generous, Sensuous and Quirky." The New York Times 144 (March 24, 1995): B1, B6.

————. "A Wrapped Reichstag: That's the Spirit." The New York Times 145, no. 2 (December 31, 1995): H37.

Knaff, Devorah L. "The Wrong Turn Was The Right Move." Riverside Co. Press Enterprise (August 26, 1990).

Knight, Christopher. "An Art of Darkness at MOCA." Los Angeles Times (January 28, 1992): F1, F4-5.

————. "Beneath Art's Slick, Serene Surface, Danger Lurks." Los Angeles Herald Examiner (March 25, 1988): E4.

————. "Bland View of Art Served at Biennial." Los Angeles Herald Examiner (May 7, 1989): E9-10.

————. "Charles Ray's Still Lifes." Parkett (Switzerland), no. 37 (September 1993): 46-51.

————. "Crushed by Good Intentions." Los Angeles Times (March 10, 1993): F10.

————. "Documenta 9." Los Angeles Times (July 12, 1992): 4, 84.

————. "Lots of 'Sunshine,' Little Light." Los Angeles Times Calendar (July 27, 1997): 4, 5, and 85.

————. "The Museum as Stage." Los Angeles Times (April 26, 1992): 85.

————. "Revolutionary Concept." Los Angeles Herald Examiner (March 25, 1988): E4.

————. "Sculpted Wreck Turns Gallery Patrons Into Looky-Loos." Los Angeles Times (October 28, 1997): F1, F9.

————. "Sculptor Takes Himself Out of Picture." Los Angeles Times (August 5, 1990): 103-104.

————. "Toning it Down at the Whitney." Los Angeles Times Calendar (April 16, 1995): 5, 54.

Kornblau, Gary. "Cover." Art Issues, no. 9 (February 1990): front and inside back covers.

Kotz, Liz. "Video Drone." Artforum 31, no. 9 (May 1993): 15-16.

Kung, Cieo. "An Alternative to Emptiness." Columbia Daily Spectator (February 28, 1991): 10.

Kunstadt, Theodor von. "The 1989 Whitney Biennial: A Triumphant Co-mingling of Heterogeneity and Blandness." Flash Art, no. 147 (Summer 1989): 139.

Kuoni, Gisela. "Charles Ray in Zurich und Bern." Bundner Zeitung (September 9, 1994): 27.

Kuspit, Donald. "The Decline, Fall and Magical Resurrection of the Body." Sculpture (May-June 1994): 20-23.

Kyander, Pontus. "Arte & Cuerpo." Heterogenesis, no. 7 (April 1994): 53.

Levin, Kim. "Art in Brief." The Village Voice (May 12, 1992): 77.

————. "Choices." The Village Voice (May 16, 1989): 48.

Lewis, Ben. "Minimalist House of Horrors." The Pink Paper (November 3, 1990).

Loock, Ulrich. "Charles Ray: Eroffnung am 27. August, Dauer bis 9. Oktober." Berner Kunstmittleilungen (Switzerland), no. 296 (September-October 1994): 3-4.

Mack, Gerhard. "Puppen, Sex und Wurfelspiel." Cash-Schweiz (September 2, 1994): 90-91.

————. "Puppen und Wurfel: Die Kunsthallen in Bern und Zürich zeigen das spektakulare Werk von Charles Ray." Suddeutsche Zeitung (September 18, 1994): 14.

Maloney, Martin. "Young Americans: Parts I & II." Flash Art 29, no. 188 (May-June 1996): 108-109.

Marincola, Paula. "Philadelphia: Prisons, Temples, and Other Alternative Spaces." Art News 94, no. 8 (October 1995): 61-62.

McFadden, David. "Stephen Schofield, Charles Ray." Vanguard (Canada) (Summer 1985).

McKenna, Kristine. "It Happens Every Two Years." Los Angeles Times Calendar (March 9, 1997): 3, 78.

Melrod, George "New York." Sculpture (July-August 1993): 55-56.

Morgan, Anne Barclay. "Donald and Mera Rubell." Sculpture (May-June 1996): 16-17.

Morgan, Stuart. "Body Language." frieze (September-October 1992): 30-31.

Muchnic, Suzanne. 'Art in the City of Angels and Demons." Los Angeles Times Sunday Calendar (January 26, 1992): 4-5.

————. "Art Windfall." Los Angeles Times (January 30, 1997): A1, A21.

————. 'The Galleries." Los Angeles Times (March 11, 1988): 23.

————. 'Charles Ray: Sculpture." Art News 92, no. 9 (November 1993): 125-26.

Myers, Terry R. "Charles Ray." Flash Art, no. 148 (October 1989): 134.

"New York and the Opening of 'Charles Ray.'" The Contemporary (The Museum of Contemporary Art, Los Angeles) (Spring 1998): 10.

Nilsson, John Peter. "Charles Ray." Kunst-Bulletin (Switzerland) (September 1994): 12-17.

————. "Charles Ray at Rooseum." Flash Art 27, no. 126 (May 1994): 124-125.

————. "To break and to push against." Siksi (Finland), no. 2 (June 1994): 14-15

Norklun, Kathi. "Run That By Me Again?" Spectacle, no. 2 (1984): 3-4.

Obejas, Achy. "Tub of Art." The Reader (May 1, 1987): 53-54.

Oberholzer, Von N klaus. "Ientitatsfragen—vom Spiel bis zur Horrorvision: Die Kunsthallen von Bern und Zürich zeigen die Plastiken des Amerikaners Charles Ray." Luzerner Zeitung (August 30, 1994): 30.

O'Brien, John. "Charles Ray." New Art Examiner 18, no. 4 (December 1990): 40.

Pagel, David. "Charles Ray." Art Issues, no. 23 (May-June 1992): 32-33.

————. "Charles Ray." Forum International (Belgium) 13, no. 3 (May-August 1992): 79-82.

————. "Charles Ray." Arts Magazine 65, no. 2 (October 1990): 104.

————. "Vexed Sex." Art Issues, no. 9 (February 1990): 11-16.

Palmer, Laurie. "Charles Ray." Artforum 26, no. 8 (April 1988): 153.

"Permanent Collection: New Acquistions." The Contemporary (The Museum of Contemporary Art, Los Angeles) (Spring 1997): 10-11.

Pincus, Robert. "Charles Ray brings art out of the Ordinary." San Diego Union (July 29, 1990): E2-3.

————. "Quality Material...: Duchamp Disseminated in the Sixties and Seventies." West Coast Duchamp (1991): 99.

————. "Room for Improvement in This Show." Los Angeles Times (November 6, 1984): 5.

Plagens, Peter. "We come to Manson High." Newsweek 119, no. 9 (March 2, 1992): 65-66.

Politi, Giancarlo, and Helena Kontova. "Post-Human: Jeffrey Deitch's Brave New Art." Flash Art 25, no. 167 (November-December 1992): 66-68.

Puvogel, Renate. "Wilhelm Schurmann: Dauer Im Wechsel." Artis (July-August): 40-45.

Ray, Charles. "Four Artists." Forehead 2 (1987): 82-99.

————. "The Most Beautiful Woman in the World." Parkett (Switzerland), no. 37 (September 1993): 52-53.

————. "New Work." New Orleans Review (Summer 1980): 180-182.

————. "A Portfolio." Forehead 1 (1987): 86-90.

————. "A Text." Spazio Umano/Human Space (Milan) 1 (January 1988): 47-57.

————. Spazio Umano/Human Space 4 (April 1989): 139-160.

Ray, Charles, and Franz West: A Collaboration, Parkett (Switzerland), no. 37 (September 1993): 16-17.

Rankin-Reid, Jane. "Still Trauma." Flash Art, no. 146 (May-June 1989).

Relyea, Lane. "Charles Ray: In the No." Artforum 31, no. 1 (September 1992): 62-66 and front cover.

————. "Charles Ray in the No." Bijutsu Techo (Japan) (April 1993): 184-194.

Rian, Jeff. "Biennale de Lyon: The Other." Flash Art 30, no. 196 (October 1997): 94-95.

————. "Past Sense, Present Sense." Artscribe International (Great Britain), no. 73 (January-February 1989): 60-65.

————. "What's all this body Art?" Flash Art 26, no. 168 (January-February 1993): 50-53.

Rice, Robin. "PerForms: Janine Antoni, Charles Ray, Jana Sterbak." Philadelphia City Paper (September 22-29, 1995): 23.

Rinder, Lawrence. "The Sculpture of Charles Ray." University Art Museum Calendar (Berkeley) (November-December 1990): 4.

Rugoff, Ralph. "MOCA Gets Nasty: Helter Skelter and the Art of Our Times." L.A. Weekly (January 31-February 6, 1992): 19-25.

————. "The Show of Shows." Harper's Bazaar, no. 3400 (March 1995): 332-337.

Saltz, Jerry. "L.A. Rising." Art & Auction 16, no. 9 (April 1994): 88-91, 122.

Salvioni, Daniela. "Feature Gallery." Flash Art, no. 140 (May-June 1988): 97.

Saunders, Wade. "Los Angeles." Bomb (Winter 1988): 102-115.

Schjeldahl, Peter. "Beauty is Back." The New York Times Magazine (September 29, 1996): 161.

————. "The Documenta of the Dog." Art in America 80, no. 9 (September 1992): 88-97.

————. "Missing: The Pleasure Principal." The Village Voice (March 16, 1993): 34, 38.

————. "The Muses on Strike." 7 Days 2, no. 19 (May 17, 1989): 67, 69.

————. "One Man Show: Klaus Kertess's Biennial 'Moyen sensuel.'" The Village Voice (April 1995).

————. "Ray's Tack." Parkett (Switzerland), no. 37 (September 1993): 18-28.

————. "Think Box." The Village Voice (March 5, 1991): 77.

Schorr, Collier. "A Pose is a Pose is a Pose: Fashion and Art and Fashion." frieze, no. 33 (March-April 1997): 60-65.

Selwyn, Marc. "Talk of the Trade: Best in the Show." Art & Auction 11, no. 2 (September 1988): 60-69.

————. "New Art L.A." Flash Art, no. 141 (Summer 1988): 109-115. Interview.

Sheikh, Simon. "Art Reviews: Sunshine & Noir." Art/Text, no. 59 (November 1997-January 1998): 84.

Smith, Richard. "Tradition and Transition in Southern California Art." New Art Examiner 16, no. 7 (March 1989): 25-28.

# Bibliography

Smith, Roberta. "Art That Hails From the Land of Deja Vu." The New York Times 138, no. 2 (June 4, 1989): C34.

———. "At The Whitney, A Biennial With a Social Conscience" The New York Times 142 (March 5, 1993): C1, C27.

———. "Body, Body Everywhere, Whole and Fragmented." The New York Times 141 (May 15, 1992): C24.

———. "Turning the Corner on Political Correctness?" The New York Times 140, no. 2 (March 3, 1991): H33.

Sozansk, Edward J. "An exhibition that demonstrates how less can indeed by–less." The Philadelphia Inquirer (September 20, 1995): G2.

Steiner, Juri. "Me, Myself, and I." Zürichsee-Zeitung (Switzerland) (September 29, 1994): 8.

Stephens, Richard. "Aspects of Our Corporeal Selves." Artweek 20, no. 26 (August 12, 1989).

Storr, Robert. "All For One and One For All." Parkett (Switzerland), no. 37 (September 1993): 29-35.

"Szene Los Angeles: Charles Ray." Art das Kunstmagazin (December 1997): 39.

Tobler, Konrad. "Staunen über verschobène Sinnbezuge." Berner Zeitung (Switzerland) (August 27, 1994): 22.

Toderi, Grazia. "Documenta IX." Flash Art (Italian Edition) 25 (1992): 56-59 and front cover.

———. "Four Brief Stories About Bodies (Alienated, Doubled, Mutated and at Rest)." Flash Art 25, no. 166 (October 1992): 133-134.

Trenkler, Thomas. "Leichtgewicht and Schwanengesang." Wirtschafts Woche (Austria) (June 25, 1992): 68-70.

Trudeau, Garry. "Doonesbury Cartoon." Los Angeles Times (1986): 18.

Tumlir, Jan. "Charles Ray." Art Issues, no. 24 (November 1990): 30.

Vangelisti, Paul. "Relating Appearances and Realities." Artweek 19, no. 12 (March 26, 1988): 5.

Verzotti, Giorgio. 'Charles Ray." Artforum 33, no. 6 (February 1995): 99.

Vine, Richard. "Report from Denmark: Part I: Louisiana Techno-Rave." Art in America 84, no. 10 (October 1996): 41-47.

Vinoles, Pepe. "La exagerada realidad." Liberación cultural (March 11, 1994): 4-5.

Vogel, Carol. "Ins de Art." The New York Times (January 3, 1997): B18.

Von Petra, Kipphoff. "Der Körper, die Teile, die Orte, die Reste." Die Zeit (June 19, 1992): 58.

Wakefield, Neville. "Out on a Limb." British Vogue (July 1994): 32.

Watkins, Eileen. "Rutgers artists throw housewarming party." The Star Ledger (March 20, 1996): 39, 50.

Weinraub, Bernard. "Art and the Underside of Los Angeles." The New York Times 141 (March 4, 1992): B1 and B4.

Zwez, Annelise. "Das Leiden an Luge und Wahrheit." Colothurner Zeitung (September 22, 1994): 29.

# WORKS IN THE EXHIBITION

Untitled, 1973
Black-and-white photograph mounted on rag board
20½ x 42½ in.
Edition of 7, 2 A.P.
The Museum of Contemporary Art, Los Angeles
Gift of Lannan Foundation

Plank Piece I-II, 1973
Two black-and-white photographs mounted on rag board
39½ x 27 in. each
Edition of 7, 2 A.P.
The Museum of Contemporary Art, Los Angeles
Gift of Lannan Foundation

All My Clothes, 1973
Sixteen Kodachrome photographs mounted on board
9 x 60 in.
Edition of 12
The Museum of Contemporary Art, Los Angeles
Gift of Lannan Foundation

Untitled (Glass Chair), 1976 (1989)
Wood and glass
37 x 72 x 72 in.
Collection Florence and Philippe Segalot
Exhibition copy courtesy Brian D. Butler

Viral Research, 1986
Plexiglas, steel, ink
32 x 53 x 36 in.
Collection Re Rebaudengo Sandretto

How a Table Works, 1986
Steel with metal box, thermos, plastic cup, terra cotta pot
with synthetic plant, painted metal can
44 x 46 x 32 in.
The Museum of Contemporary Art, Los Angeles
Gift of Lannan Foundation

Tub with Black Dye, 1986
Tub, glass, test tubes, pipe, dye
33 ½ x 59 x 30 in.
Collection of United Yarn Products, Inc., New Jersey

Ink Box, 1986
Steel, ink, automobile paint
36 x 36 x 36 in.
Orange County Museum of Art, Newport Beach, California: Museum
purchase with additional funds provided by Edward R. Broida

Ink Line, 1987
Ink
Dimensions variable
The Museum of Contemporary Art, Los Angeles
Gift of the artist

Rotating Circle, 1988
Electric motor with 9 in. diameter disc
9 in. in diameter
Edition of 3
The Museum of Contemporary Art, Los Angeles
Gift of Lannan Foundation

Bath, 1989
Porcelain bathtub, brass, aluminum, water
60 x 29½ x 21 in.
The Museum of Contemporary Art, Los Angeles
The El Paso Natural Gas Company Fund for California Art

32x33x35=34x33x35, 1989
Aluminum
Interior: 34 x 33 x 35 in.
Exterior: 32 x 33 x 35 in.
Collection of Mark Jancou

Tabletop, 1988
Wood table with ceramic plate, metal canister, plastic bowl,
plastic tumbler, aluminum shaker, terra cotta pot, plant, motor
43 x 52½ x 35 in.
The Museum of Contemporary Art, Los Angeles
Gift of Lannan Foundation

Self-Portrait, 1990
Mixed media
75 x 26 x 20 in.
Orange County Museum of Art, Newport Beach, California

7½-ton Cube, 1990
Steel and automobile paint
36 x 36 x 36 in.
Collection of Re Rebaudengo Sandretto

Table, 1990
Plexiglas and steel
35⅜ x 35⅜ x 52¾ in.
Edition of 3
Collection of Mardy and Clifford Einstein

Male Mannequin, 1990
Mixed media
73½ x 15 x 14 in.
Edition of 3
The Eli Broad Family Foundation, Santa Monica;
Courtesy Gagosian Gallery, New York and Los Angeles

Yes, 1990
Framed color photograph, convex wall
51¼ x 44 x ½ in.
Galerie Hauser & Wirth, Zurich

Fall '91, 1992
Mixed media
96 x 26 x 36 in.
The Museum of Contemporary Art, Los Angeles
Promised gift of Eileen and Peter Norton

Fall '91, 1992
Mixed media
96 x 26 x 36 in.
The Eli Broad Family Foundation, Santa Monica;
Courtesy Gagosian Gallery, New York and Los Angeles

Fall '91, 1992
Mixed media
96 x 26 x 36 in.
Collection of Dakis Joannou

No, 1992
Color photograph in artist's frame
38 x 30 in.
Edition of 4
The Museum of Contemporary Art, Los Angeles
Gift of Lannan Foundation

Boy, 1992
Painted fiberglass, steel, fabric
71½ x 27 x 34 in.
Edition of 3
Whitney Museum of American Art; Purchase with funds from Jeffrey
Deitch, Bernardo Nacal-Ginard, and Penny and Mike Winton

Oh! Charley, Charley, Charley…, 1992
Mixed media
72 x 180 x 180 in
Rubell Family Collections

Firetruck, 1993
Painted aluminum, fiberglass, Plexiglas
12 x 8 x 46½ ft.
The Eli Broad Family Foundation, Santa Monica;
Courtesy Gagosian Gallery, New York and Los Angeles

Family Romance, 1993
Mixed media
53 x 96 x 24 in.
Edition of 3
Collection of Eileen and Peter Norton

Poster for Ray exhibition
at the Kunsthallen Bern/Zürch, 1994
Poster
39½ x 27⅝ in.
Collection of the artist

Puzzle Bottle, 1995
Glass, painted wood, cork
13⅜ x 3¾ x 3¾ in.
Whitney Museum of American Art, New York; Purchase, with funds
from the Contemporary Painting and Sculpture Committee, and
Barbara and Eugene Schwartz

Fashions, 1996
16 mm film, 12 min., color
Collection of the artist

Unpainted Sculpture, 1997
Fiberglass and paint
60 x 78 x 171 in.
Walker Art Center, Minneapolis; Gift of Bruce and Martha Atwater,
Ann and Barrie Birks, Dolly Fiterman, Erwin and Miriam Kelen, Larry
Perlman and Linda Peterson Perlman, Harriet and Edson Spencer
with additional funds from the T.B. Walker Acquisition Fund, 1998

Self-portrait with Homemade Clothes, 1998
35 mm film, 4 min., color, sound
Courtesy of the artist and Cornelia Grassi

## PHOTO CREDITS

All images courtesy of the artist, or institution listed in the caption unless otherwise noted below.
Cover: Caro, courtesy Tate Gallery London; Ray, photo by Joshua White
Feto Pedrini, pp. 3, 6, 8, 17, 18, 22, 23, 25, 31, 34-35, 37; Susan Einstein, pp. 4-5, 67, 69; Courtesy Donald Young Gallery, Seattle, pp. 28, 46;
Peter Muscato, pp. 29, 37; Photograph © 1998 The Museum of Modern Art, New York, pp. 38-39; Reprinted with permission, © Newsday, Inc.,
1997 p. 41; Courtesy of Regen Projects, p. 44; © 1998: Whitney Museum of American Art, New York, p. 47; Joshua White, pp. 48-49, 90, 94, 100
(top and bottom); Copyright Greydon Wood, 1994, Philadelphia Museum of Art, p.68; Marcus J. Leith, p. 42-43, 88; Courtesy Museum
of Contemporary Art, Tokyo, p. 97 top (photo © Shigeo Anzaï); © 1998 Whitney Museum of American Art, New York, p. 99 both, 102 (photo:
Geoffrey Clements p. 99 both), (photo: Jerry L. Thompson p. 102); © 1998 Andy Warhol Foundation for the Visual Arts / ARS, New York, p. 101.

### EDITORS
Russell Ferguson and Stephanie Emerson
Editorial Assistant: Jane Hyun
### DESIGN
Lorraine Wild and Amanda Washburn
### PRINTING
Dr. Cantz'sche Druckerei, Germany

Copublished by The Museum of Contemporary Art, Los Angeles
and Scalo Verlag, Zurich.

Copyright © 1998 The Museum of Contemporary Art, Los Angeles
250 South Grand Avenue, Los Angeles, California 90012

ISBN 0-914357-59-X

### LIBRARY OF CONGRESS
#### CATALOGUING-IN-PUBLICATION DATA

Ray Charles, 1953-
  Charles Ray / organized by Paul Schimmel; with essays
by Paul Schimmel and Lisa Phillips.
       p.    cm.
  Catalog of an exhibition held at the Museum of
Contemporary Art, Los Angeles, Nov. 15, 1998-Feb. 21, 1999.
  Includes bibliographical references.
  ISBN 0-914357-59-X (cloth)
  1. Ray, Charles, 1953-  --Exhibitions.  I. Schimmel, Paul.
  II. Phillips, Lisa. III. Museum of Contemporary Art
(Los Angeles, Calif.) IV. Title.
N6537.R29A4 1998
730'.92--dc21                                98-22452
                                                  CIP